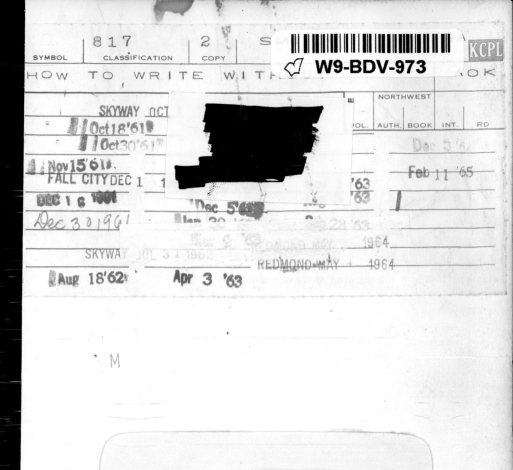

Books by H. ALLEN SMITH

MR. KLEIN'S KAMPF

LOW MAN ON A TOTEM POLE

LIFE IN A PUTTY KNIFE FACTORY

LOST IN THE HORSE LATITUDES

RHUBARB

LO, THE FORMER EGYPTIAN!

LARKS IN THE POPCORN

WE WENT THATAWAY

PEOPLE NAMED SMITH

MISTER ZIP

SMITH'S LONDON JOURNAL

THE COMPLEAT PRACTICAL JOKER

THE REBEL YELL

THE AGE OF THE TAIL

WRITE ME A POEM, BABY

THE PIG IN THE BARBER SHOP

DON'T GET PERCONEL WITH A CHICKEN

WAIKIKI BEACHNIK

HOW TO WRITE WITHOUT KNOWING NOTHING

Selected by H. Allen Smith

DESERT ISLAND DECAMERON

With Ira L. Smith

LOW AND INSIDE

THREE MEN ON THIRD

*HOW TO WRITE
WITHOUT KNOW-
ING NOTHING*

H. Allen Smith

HOW TO WRITE WITHOUT KNOW-ING NOTHING

A Book Largely Concerned with the Use and Misuse of Language at Home and Abroad

 Boston  Toronto

LITTLE, BROWN AND COMPANY

I AM by reputation a humorist. That is, I am classified as a humorist by a certain culture group composed of people who think I write funny. Ranged against this opinion are whole populations who look upon me as a smart aleck. This is a condition of life that all humorists must accept, for there is a thin wavering line separating the humorist from the smart aleck. I think that all of us stagger and fall across that line now and then.

A humorist has a greater concern with words than do writers in other categories, for much of his fun is drawn out of the manner in which he constructs his phrases, distorts his sentences, and rides his words off in all directions. Mark Twain was by no means the last person to observe that American humor doesn't stand up under translation. True enough, translations of Mark Twain are widely popular in the Soviet Union, but I think it likely that the Russians admire him for his iconoclasm, for his continuing blasts against orthodoxy, for his steady irreverence toward certain aspects of the American way, rather than for his humor alone.

I think I can illustrate my point by recalling the career of a man named F. Chase Taylor, who was known to the American radio audience in the 1930's as Colonel Lemuel Q. Stoopnagle.

He was a *method* humorist and wrote his own material and I had the privilege of working with him for a while about twenty-five years ago when he was at the peak of his popularity. (Later in this book you will find some examples of the Colonel's technique.) Much of his comedy was based on his way with words, his ability to manipulate the English language into odd and fantastic patterns. One of his most quoted lines was, "People have more fun than anybody." I would like to offer a sentence of similar grace and beauty to set the mood for this scholarly work: "Words can be funnier than everything." This is still true in the 1960's in spite of a public utterance to the contrary, public utteranced by Dr. Mason W. Gross, president of Rutgers University, a man of exuberant spirit and wit, endowed with a mustache. Dr. Gross spoke as follows:

I think it could safely be said that of all the billions of words that are poured forth every single day in this country, not more than a handful are used as words should be used. All the fun seems to be gone out of words. We have become ponderous, inexact, clumsy, and totally without humor in our approach to our most precious of possessions. We recently had a candidate for the presidency of the United States who showed some delight in the use of words, but he was criticized for treating high office with levity and jokes. The notion that wit is a mark of high intelligence seems to be frowned upon. . . . Somehow in the midst of the greatest tide of words that the world has ever known, we have become suspicious of words, and we use them not to convey meaning, or ideas, or humor, or delight, but rather as heavy, clumsy and dull marks of respectability and unreason. We love the sound of our own voices, *ad nauseam,* but we hate words . . . we don't want our words to have any meanings, to play any tricks, to have any life, or to say anything new.

This book has been in the planning stage for at least ten years and was not projected as an answer to Dr. Gross. It is concerned, in large part, with the fun that can be had from the use and misuse of language, spoken as well as written. Its purpose is to entertain the reader although, as is usual with my books, the dis-

viii

cerning person will find brilliant and subtle philosophical observations half-concealed behind the clowning and the smart-aleck-
ing. I can't help this. Somehow, in spite of unshirted hell, the
wisdom seems to creep into my stuff. This is saddening to me,
for all I want from life is truth and beauty and money.

— H. ALLEN SMITH

CONTENTS

xii

HOW TO WRITE WITHOUT KNOW- ING NOTHING

1. PLEASE PASS THE COCAINE

BACK IN THE pre-Jurassic period when I was a young man (playing me a waiting game), I had an assortment of ridiculous ambitions. The wildest of these was the yearning to become the author of a book. I knew it was impossible, but I put my shoulder to the wheel (invented during the preceding year) and worked for two decades and finally made it.

My first two books were quite modest in their scope and less than that in their acceptance by the public, but they were books and they had my name on their covers. By the time I had written them I already knew that the only way to learn to write is to write, and then write some more, and keep on writing with a steadfast fury year after year after year. And to spend an hour or two every day studying — reading classics and biographies and histories, especially histories, because history properly written covers the whole scope of human life, including human folly, in which I am a devout believer.

I am congenitally slothful, and I've always been inclined to steady merrymaking, so it was a rough job for me to do all this. Still, I did it. I kept on writing in my spare time and finally turned out a book that attracted a lot of attention, and leaped to the top of the best-seller lists, and even brought me soul-stirring compliments from such heroic characters as Damon Runyon and H. L. Mencken and Gene Fowler.

In the days when I first took down with *cacoethes scribendi* — the irresistible itch to write — the people who were turning out successful books were, of all things, writers. They were pros. The aforementioned H. L. Mencken, and Sinclair Lewis, Theodore Dreiser, Sherwood Anderson, H. G. Wells, Booth Tarkington, Somerset Maugham — these were the glittering stars who dominated the best-seller lists, along with people like Zane Grey and Mary Roberts Rinehart and Rex Beach and Harold Bell Wright and Kathleen Norris. All professional writers, no matter how great or how small their talent.

Then the non-writers began to take over the business of writing. Henry Ford didn't write his autobiography, *My Life and Work,* which he wrote in 1922. Trader Horn wrote his best-selling book in 1927, and it was written by Ethelreda Lewis. Lindbergh turned out *We* the same year without touching a pencil. A fine upstanding American character named Gaston Means wrote a scandalous book in 1930, although he didn't write it. From then on things began to snowball. Influential men and women in various prominent callings got out of bed in the morning, yawned, scratched their navels, and said, "Say. I wonder how it would be to be a writer. Think I'd like it. Guess I'll try it." So they shopped around and found a real writer in need of rent and gin money and they secretly hired that writer to write them a book. After a while the tiniest bit of demi-integrity got into the game, and the "as-told-to" books began rolling off the presses. There are plenty of them today, but there are also plenty of books by non-writers whose publishers put forward strong claims that they were actually written, sentence after sentence, by the celebrity. The louder they make these claims, the more positive it becomes that a professional writer had a hand in production of the book. One movie

4

actor's autobiography, recently a best-seller, was issued with such a claim, iterated and reiterated. He actually wrote it, cried the publisher. With his own hot little hands. Every last word of it. They kept yelling and kept yelling and then somebody quietly did a bit of investigation and found out that the actor's own hot little hands were in his pants pockets, or in the pants pockets of assorted concupiscent broads. The book was written by a talented hack. I am somewhat reminded of the remark made about television by the late Fred Allen: "The atmosphere is the same as if somebody had dropped a loaded privy into the air-conditioning system."

I remember a few years back when a minor-league lady author sued a leading comedian, charging that he engaged her to write a novel under his name so he could acquire a reputation as a literary man. The judge threw the case out, saying that the transaction between author and comedian was not actionable because, basically, it was a fraud on the public. Just recently this same comedian's name appeared as co-author of a novel. He and all of his show-biz friends, who are legion, appeared on dozens of television and radio shows boosting his book, rarely ever mentioning the professional writer who was his "collaborator" and who, I'm bound to believe, really did the writing.

I know about another top actor-comedian who, some years back, became the author of a best-seller. His book was written in the publisher's office with very little contact between principal and ghost, and then was submitted to the comedian for approval. His verdict was: "My God, what a swell book I've written!" I used to be friendly with a wealthy show-business personality who one day decided that *he* wanted to be a writer. He went out and hired a whole stable of boys, capable but hungry writers, and put them to work, and before long my friend was being quoted wide and far as a great wit and humorist. This gave me a slow burn, which in time became a fast burn, and one day I said to him, "You may not realize it, but you are taking dollars out of my pocket. I have a humor book in the stores and you have a humor book in the stores, but you are a wealthy man and you are laying out large sums of your own money to boost the advertising budget on your book. Why the hell can't you be satisfied with being what you are? Why do you have to buy yourself a reputation as an author?" He asked me to leave his baronial premises and our relations came to an end.

I may, at last, be approaching the point of this whole discussion. I have spent something like thirty-five years trying to learn to be a competent writer. Some people believe I have achieved my aim. Yet today I find myself, along with many other writers whose careers match my own, being pushed off the best-seller lists by a lot of writers who are not writers. Any comic who enjoys public favor automatically writes a book, which he is incapable of writing. These boys are horrible hams, but they are also skilled practitioners of the hard sell. They race from one TV show to the next, thrusting a copy of their fraudulent book into the eye of the camera. One publisher admitted recently that the jackets of his books are now designed with eye-catching type, the better to be seen when rammed down the public's throat on television shows. And I actually heard one comedian, shoving his book forward, say on a TV show: "Folks, I want you to know that this is a real swell book. All my friends say so, and it is a best-seller like crazy, and you're bound to get a real charge out of it. So go out and buy a copy because you will never have so much fun in your life."

One night somebody on a television show asked Dody Goodman, the girl who undertakes the role of amiable idiot, if she had started writing a book yet. "No," she said. "They asked me to write a book but all the subjects have been used up."

There are up-from-degradation books, some by gutter-drunk actresses who have taken the veil, others by ex-hopheads, whether they be boxers or radio announcers or mildewed beat-

6

niks. There are books by fat lady parasites living off the soft underbelly of big-ess Society whether in Washington or New York or Europe. There are books by rapists occupying death cells, and by junkies who play bop music, and by countless semiliterate politicians who draw upon the huge pool of ghost writers operating in Washington in order that they, the politicians, may become eloquent and graceful in their prose. There are books by preachers who know the solutions to all human problems but who couldn't locate their collarbones with both hands, by guys who tell how they made forty million dollars with one arm tied behind their backs, by drunken fliers and by lawyers whose ethics would offend the sensitive soul of Frank Costello, and by arrogant tennis players and by advertising executives seeking to establish some justification for their humbuggery and by doctors who want the human race to cure its ills by dosing itself with a mixture of goat's milk and persimmon juice. There are books galore by television personalities famous for their petulance or their insolence toward their guests, hence national heroes. There are books by celebrated keepers of bawdyhouses and by whiny crack-note singers not old enough to work up a sweat in the armpits. Please remember that when the former truck driver, Elvis Presley, arrived home from service in the army, he was asked about his plans, and his first response, delivered in all seriousness, was: "I'm a-gonna write a book." He was inspired, no doubt, by the tremendous literary success of another singer in the seedtime of life, one Pat Boone, philosopher. Either that or by the fact that a successful book in recent years was written by Lassie, the dog. As told to a man named Rudd Weatherwax. Honest to God.

As I say, all of this has been somewhat depressing to me. Well, not exactly depressing. Infuriating. In a recent book for children a lady author included a chapter, "How to Write a Book." She said: "You can write a book about anything . . . If you can't write yet, you could just draw. Then the book

7

could be for someone who can't read yet. Or you could write a book for someone who can read only one word."

I think it's coming to that. I used to believe that book publishers were people in a very special sort of business governed by a very special set of ethics. They held themselves aloof from the toils and stratagems and outright buccaneering of the business community. But today I suspect that some of them are interested in . . . well, in m-o-n-e-y. They will publish any book. A semiliterate TV performer submits a book to them and they give no thought to the quality of its contents — their interest is solely in the size of his audience and his willingness to plug himself blue in the face.

Such being the case, it is understandable why more and more non-writers are busy writing into tape recorders. I am continually astounded at the caliber of people I meet who think they can write. They are a multitude and it never occurs to them that a certain amount of training would be helpful as preliminary to a writing career. In this connection I would like to digress for a moment. I have become convinced that I have the physical appearance and the conversational ability of John J. Kallikak. Perhaps a few cuts below him. Week after week I meet new people, some in the country, some in the city, and I note that they study me curiously, and later I find out that they have gone home and started writing. It is quite clear what inspired them. They looked at me and they said to themselves, "Well, if that funny-looking kook can make a living as a writer, then *I* ought to become a millionaire as a writer." They come back to me eventually, of course, with their grubby out-of-kilter manuscripts, single-spaced and smudged and aswarm with misspellings and grammatical atrocities, and they offer me a percentage of the take if I'll dress the stuff up and get it published. I strangle them.

All of this leads me to say that I believe, logical or not, that if a man is incapable of writing a book, he should not be permitted to set himself up as a writer, to pass himself off as an author. There is such a thing as too much freedom of the press. I believe that, with a handful of exceptions, nobody ever said, out of a clear sky or even a cloudy one, "I guess I'll be a writer," and became one immediately.

What can I do about it?

Nothing.

Except, perhaps, I could inaugurate a whole new career — as a drug addict. I hear it makes you feel good.

And now that I am off to such a temperate and tolerant and good-natured beginning, let us get on with the business at hand.

₩₩₩₩₩₩₩₩₩₩₩₩₩₩₩₩₩₩₩₩₩₩₩₩₩₩₩

2. LEAVE MY NERVOUS
TENSION ALONE

₩₩₩₩₩₩₩₩₩₩₩₩₩₩₩₩₩₩₩₩₩₩₩₩₩₩₩

FOR SOME REASON that isn't quite clear to me, the lady of my house became involved, not long ago, in an organization dedicated to the conquest of mental illness. She began in a minor way with a local group, then was recruited into the county mental health organization and the next thing I heard she was chairman of this and vice-president of that and a member of the board of directors. Several times lately I have caught her in the act of staring at me as if she'd known me somewhere before.

To my way of thinking these activities amount to a heartless conspiracy against me, aimed at putting me out of business. Given a population in which everyone is in robust health mentally (instead of the precise opposite, as now), it will be necessary for me to retire to Hawaii and sit in the sun, studying the twitching and vibrating fannies of brown-skinned gals. I could never, of course, bring myself to that.

9

The thing began to weigh upon me and then one morning I went into a slump. Arriving at my desk I squared off in front of the typewriter and in forty-five seconds I was bruxing, i.e., grinding my teeth. I felt as if my head had been caught in one of those paint-shakers they have in hardware stores. The words just wouldn't come. I was in the grip of a seizure known technically as *writer's block*. The term is defined ordinarily as meaning a period in a writer's week or month when he is unable to get a single satisfactory sentence on paper. It corresponds to a ballplayer's batting slump except perhaps in the matter of duration. I have known writers who have gone into slumps that have lasted for six months or longer. It is an unhappy condition for them, for they tend to grow even wilder and more violent than in their productive periods. A flamboyant fury often possesses them and they slash and kick at living things, including vegetation. I, myself, during a long slump a couple of summers ago, picked up a scantling and struck a rose.

It seems to be a fact that more writers are suffering from more slumps today than ever before in the long and honorable history of the obligative mood. It isn't because all of their wives have gone into mental health work. I know one author who fell into a fearful slump because he wanted to go to the Kentucky Derby and couldn't.

The true reason behind all this trouble is that writers are crazy.

They have always been crazy, as any literary biography out of the past will clearly demonstrate. In former times they didn't even suspect that they were insane, but nowadays they are working, or trying to work, under the shadow of psychoanalysis and mental health crusades. They are constantly being reminded of their lunacy. This might conceivably be a good thing for the generality of citizens, but it's sheer poison for authors.

The psychoanalysts themselves seem to have made an important discovery in recent years; that to scratch a writer —

any writer — is to find a nut. The doctors are writing books about writers. They are turning out articles about the writing profession in general and about individual maniacs engaged in it. They are reviewing books in the Sunday supplements and in the literary journals. More and more they are stretching authors on their couches and asking them to talk about their mamas. And on top of everything else, we now have our general practitioners hurling tranquilizing pills indiscriminately around the landscape. As the politicians say, America is strong and vital and vigorous and dynamic — standing serenely confident before the rest of the kooky world. Last year we gobbled down more than six hundred tons of tranquilizers.

The fact that writers are measurably crazier than any other group has been suspected for centuries, but the writers themselves didn't really know about it until the Era of the Analyst — a cultural epoch corresponding to the Age of Count Down (known to some social historians as the Middle Comic Book Period). Whereas a literary person formerly was content to announce, without bleeding, that he was in one of his slumps (which he sometimes cured by going out and getting majestically drunk), he now says that he is suffering from a twisted id. The old-fashioned word "slump" has vanished from his vocabulary; he says he is undergoing the agony of creative sterility, and revolvers have to be kept away from him.

There seems to be no way for a writer to escape this blight; it falls upon him whether he becomes a customer of the analysts or not. It comes at him from the printed page and it comes at him in the conversation of his friends and associates and, in time, he arrives at the conclusion that the chief tools of his trade are, (1) a typewriter, (2) a sheet of paper, and (3) a condition of imbecility. And he realizes that while he, personally, may resist to the end and escape the couch, the *stuff he turns out* may well be the medium through which the analysts get at his clabbered mind.

11

In books and in literary journals the psychiatrists are making slanderous statements about authors who have been dead for half a century or longer. The doctor sits down and analyzes Chapter Six in a novel a hundred years old and proves that the author of that novel went around imploring people to let him bite them on the toes. From three short paragraphs written in the time of John Quincy Adams and describing an unhemingwayish conversation between a boy and a girl comes the shocking revelation that the gentleman who wrote those paragraphs had dreams about falling out of Ferris wheels and believed himself capable of giving milk.

Beneath the spell of all this psychic probing our present-day authors seem unwilling to put up a fight. They refuse to defend their God-given right to run mentally amok. A prominent New York book publisher sat at lunch the other day groaning about the number of his authors who have delivered themselves body and soul into the hands of the analysts. He cited specific cases — successful writers who were spending all their royalties and most of their time on analysts. The important point, he emphasized, is that these people have either ceased producing altogether or the stuff they do write is unpublishable.

"One of these days," said the publisher wistfully, "a guy will come along with a brand new technique — he's going to de-analyze authors. He ought to become rich and famous, and I'm going to be for him and send him a lot of customers."

It's not alone the professional psychiatrists who are engaged in analyzing authors from the stuff they write. Many of the fledgling intellectuals in our colleges are acquiring a smattering of knowledge about psychoanalysis and sublimation and setch. These kids don't ever read a book for enjoyment — they psychoanalyze the author of it. I know this from personal experience, having in recent years been thrown into the company of quite a few college kids. They sit around my living room, drink

12

my beer, and leer knowingly at me. They tell me things about my mama and papa that I didn't know before. They use words that I don't know *yet*. Worst of all, they tell me that I ought to hop right down to a good analyst and have myself done over.

The implication is unmistakable that I am barmy and because of it I find myself now and then brooding lightly over my madness, even taking inventory, searching out symptoms of my own derangement.

Yet, up to now the head-shrinkers have had to get along without my trade. For fifteen years people have been telling me I ought to go. But I have resisted because one thing has been clear to me from the beginning — a writer has *got* to be crazy. That goes for T. S. Eliot as well as Truman Capote. You try to uncrazify him and you ruin him forever. Lop off his livelier eccentricities and he'll quit writing altogether or, worse than that, sink into the depravity of running for public office, or composing poetry.

Thus far I've had chief reference to the analysts, professional and amateur, who seem bent upon obliterating the lunacy of writers and thereby obliterating their right to a livelihood. There remains a motley clutch of elocution teachers, architects of the soul, and Caucasian yogis who are writing books and articles aimed at curing the cosmic restlessness of Twentieth Century Man. They are trying to deprive all of us of the right to worry and stew and fret and chew our nails. I, for one, wish they'd all shut up. I don't *want* to stop worrying. I don't *want* to have peace of mind. Deliver me, please, from confident living. *Leave my nervous tension alone.* Without my chronic edginess, my waspish behavior toward my fellow man, and my kaleidoscopic nightmares, I'd go nuts. I'd go nuts and I'd also go broke.

What's wrong with nightmares? Sometimes I go to bed early just to get at my horrible dreams ahead of other people. I have nightmares that provide me with far better conversational ma-

13

terial than I'd ever get out of a cruise to Tahiti or a stretch in stir. I happen to know that Robert Louis Stevenson got the story of *Dr. Jekyll and Mr. Hyde* out of a nightmare so violent that his wife thought he was throwing a fit.

I'll match my gloriously frayed nerves with those of any quivering neurotic in the country. I can think less on my feet than anybody I know. When I stand up to say a few words to an audience my nerves tighten up so fast that I know someday I'll double over with a loud snap — go into a stationary jackknife dive. When I undertake to deliver a speech I say "Uh" and then two words and then "Uh Uhh Uhhh" and then three words and then some more "Uhs" until I begin to sound like a three-piece German band. Once I said "Uhhhhhhh" and then had to turn around and ask the toastmaster, "What was I talking about just now?"

I want it that way. It makes for adventure and excitement in living. The nervous way is the good way of life. And as concerns the long hours of the night when, I am reliably informed, millions of people are as good as dead, mine is a time of intense eventfulness, a time of tumult in living, compatible color. I toss and thresh about like a TV wrestler trying to escape from a head-scissors. Then comes blessed sleep, that rips the stitches from the sleave of care which was never knit up very good in the first place. Good, wholesome, neurotic sleep — made bearable by serpents as big as the Super Chief snapping at me out of the blackness, by flying saucers with smiling bacteria at the controls.

These, then, are mine own possessions, to cherish and preserve. Marcel Proust wrote: "Everything great in the world comes from neurotics. They alone have founded our religions and composed our masterpieces. Never will the world know all it owes to them nor all that they have suffered to enrich us." After he wrote those lines Marcel Proust probably climbed into bed with all his clothes on and wearing heavy gloves, for that

14

was his custom. I think, perhaps, now that I'm finished with this chapter, I'll do the same.

3. THE CASE OF THE CRACKPOT COPY EDITOR

AFTER A MANUSCRIPT has been accepted by a book publisher it is handed over to a person known as a copy editor, usually of the female persuasion. It is her job to go through it with great diligence, correcting the author's grammatical blunders and misspellings and, wherever possible, checking all statements of fact.

About fifteen years ago I put together an anthology of humorous essays and short stories under the title *Desert Island Decameron*. It included marvelous pieces by such writers as H. L. Mencken and Mark Twain and Dorothy Parker and Roark Bradford and Fred Allen and James Street and Robert Benchley and Ben Hecht and James Thurber and Thorne Smith and Stephen Leacock and Ring Lardner.

From the works of Lardner I chose the story "Mr. Frisbie," a piece supposedly written by a naïve and artless and semi-literate fellow who served as both chauffeur and caddy for his wealthy employer. I copied "Mr. Frisbie" from a Lardner book with meticulous care; it would have been literary sacrilege if the narrator's choice of language and spelling were changed in any way.

The manuscript finally went to the publisher and in due course arrived in the hands of a copy editor. Weeks later it came back to me with galley proofs; it was now my job to read

15

these galleys and make any last-minute alterations I felt were needed.

When I came to the Mr. Frisbie chapter and started reading it in type, I was at first confused and then astonished and then astounded.

The copy editor had gone through Ring Lardner's story and carefully corrected every misspelled word, every syntactical error.

Where Lardner had written, "It was during while this brother-in-law was visiting Mr. Frisbie that I entered the last-named employee," this had been changed to, "It was while this brother-in-law was visiting Mr. Frisbie that I entered the latter's employ."

Where Lardner had it, "the ball . . . laid there burred in the deep sand," the copy editor had changed it to, "the ball . . . lay there buried in the sand."

The sentence "I am a great lover of horses flesh" was fixed up, of course. Such phrases as "brooched the subject" and "they disgust the matter" and "at your beckon call" and "a variable tyrant" were rendered into proper English. The same idiocy, all the way through.

The copy editor's work on that story was so incredible that, after the first shock, I began to laugh. And I continued laughing, off and on, for several days. I took the manuscript in and showed my editor what had happened to the prose style of Mr. Frisbie's chauffeur-caddy. I heard later that the copy editor was dismissed. I never knew who she (or he) was. I have never enjoyed seeing anyone lose a job, having gone through the process many times myself, but I must say that there was some justification for this particular firing. As the English put it, that copy editor was a bit foggy in the crumpet.

For some years afterward my editor (not the copy editor) took great enjoyment in telling the story to other people in the publishing business. He always told it as having happened to

16

another author at another publishing house. In the end he was so convinced that it did happen elsewhere that once, when he and I were on a trip, he said to me, "Did you ever hear about the time that a Ring Lardner story came in to the office of Houghton Mifflin and . . ."

You think I let him get away with it? Hell no.

♦♦♦♦♦♦♦♦♦♦♦♦♦♦♦♦♦♦♦♦♦♦♦♦♦♦♦♦♦♦

4. NOTES IN THE NIGHT

♦♦♦♦♦♦♦♦♦♦♦♦♦♦♦♦♦♦♦♦♦♦♦♦♦♦♦♦♦♦

ONE NIGHT a couple of years ago I awoke from a deep sleep, jerked from the grip of Morpheus by the most brilliant idea that ever passed through the mind of a mortal being. It was an idea of such magnitude that it took my breath away, and I lay there panting for a few moments. Then I groped for the bed light and found my pad and pencil and wrote it down.

As I scribbled, working rapidly so that I could collapse into sleep again, I grew even more convinced that this was a concept that would shake the earth, that the idea that had come to me in the night would alter the course of history and bring true and enduring beauty to the lives of men.

Finished writing it down, I snapped off the light and lay there a few moments, thinking of the riches that would be mine. I visualized the garage I'd have to build to hold all my flashy sports cars. Then I went back to sleep.

The next morning I crawled out of bed, dressed, and went down to breakfast. I had a piece of bacon in my hand when I remembered. It suddenly came back to me that I had committed a soul-stirring idea to paper during the night. I couldn't recall a thing about it; I couldn't even think of the nature of it. But I did know it was of supreme importance, and so I dropped

the bacon and rushed to get it, and this is what I found scrawled
on my pad:

> *this at time Roosevelt died*
> *see in clips — Times broch*
> *not understandable to me — to us —*
> *examine intellectual rot*
> *they mean well — maybe*
> *who they talkin about?*
> *the plumber*
> *the $5 gardner (this place will be closed*
> *all day owing to the death*
> *of our president)*
> *do something about it.*

There wasn't anything I could do about it. I read it over three
or four times, studying each line carefully, but the power and
the glory of it remained hidden. There was vast meaning and
significance in it somewhere, but it eluded me. It eludes me to
this day. I don't know the word "broch," and I don't know any
"$5 gardner," and I don't know what place is closed, and I
don't know what president is dead.

This is a thing that happens to me all the time. It used to be
that when I had these prodigious ideas in the night, I didn't
bother to write them down; I figured they were so great, so
towering, so magnificent, that I could not fail to remember
them the next morning. But always when morning came I never
could recall a single detail about them. During a period of twilight sleep I'd have one of those stupendous ideas, and the
next day I'd remember that I had had it, without remembering
the subject, and I'd go around all day in a sort of trance, trying
to coax it out of my mind, unable to think of anything else, unable to concentrate on my work. Finally I started forcing myself to make notes.

By inquiring around I've found that it happens to other people too. And it is the same way with all of us who write memos

18

in the night. We learn eventually to scratch the things down so they will not be lost to posterity. And then we learn that the things we scratch down for posterity are almost always pure nonsense.

For some years I have preserved a thing I scribbled during the night and which had me convinced, at the time I put it down, that I would be the first man in history to win *two* Nobel prizes in the same year — the prize for literature and the prize for peace — and *almost* the prize for chemistry. I wrote it down and then dozed off, thinking of my trip to Sweden and the fame that would be mine. The next morning I found on my scratch-pad:

> *insomnia for poor people*
> *think of something downstairs*
> *think of something in bathroom*
> (*powdered alum*)
> *think of something in bedroom*
> *R E T R A C E ! ! ! !*

Don't look at *me!* I only wrote it!

Perhaps the most famous example of note writing at night is that of Mrs. Amos Pinchot. Out of the blackness came a poem that impressed her as being so shiningly beautiful and so filled with wisdom that because of it she would be acclaimed as the greatest poet and the most profound thinker in all history. She wrote it down and in the morning this is how it looked:

> *Hogamus Higamus*
> *Men are Polygamous,*
> *Higamus Hogamus*
> *Women Monogamous.*

One of the most interesting night-thinkers to cross my path is a neighbor who is a vice-president of a large New York corporation where brainstorming sessions are held once a week.

19

My neighbor, in a period of sleeplessness, arrived at an idea which he believed would be of enormous benefit to his company, and so he wrote it down.

The next day he was unable to make any sense out of it. Still, he knew that there was a way of applying it to his business and he worried about it, and the next time he and his fellow executives were indulging in a session of brainstorming, he tossed it into the pot — reading it off his notes, as follows:

> *Is there any significance*
> *To the fact that my little fingers*
> *just fit my nostrils*
> *Or is it mere coincidence?*

After he read it off, a few wise looks appeared on faces around the table, but nobody offered to develop it further. Later, however, the president of the company called my friend aside and said, "That idea of yours — about the little fingers fitting in the nostrils — I think perhaps you've got hold of something there."

My friend exclaimed, "Great! Glad you think so. I felt it was important, but I just can't seem to find a concrete application for it."

And the boss replied, "Just leave it alone. It has a great potential. Let it gestate. One of these days, BAM! You'll have it."

My friend says that up to the present moment, no Bam! Yet he hasn't been cured of night notes. One of his more recent bafflers says: "German doctor — lines patients up in circle — checks 'em from his bicycle seat."

The scratching down of unintelligible night notes is a universal habit among professional writers, but I find that it also happens to sensible and well-adjusted people. Admiral William S. Sims used to tell of a memo written in the night by a famous English admiral during the First World War. This admiral had a

20

recurring dream in which he was shown the way to end the war swiftly and happily. During his sleep the admiral would see it all quite clearly, but when morning came he'd be unable to remember it. Finally he decided he would force himself to write it down in the night, and he did so, and the next day he hurried to read what he had written so he could get on with the job of ending the war. His master solution was stated in seven words:

The skin is mightier than the banana.

Raymond Loewy has designed a sliding night desk which emerges from a storage cabinet and takes up a position across his bed, so that he can work when he doesn't feel like sleeping. And someone else has invented and marketed a pencil with a tiny flashlight on it, to facilitate the taking of night notes. These inventors apparently operate on the assumption that all such notes and memos are valuable. I know that I have found scribblings on my bedside pad that almost contained wisdom, such as "She was inhuman toward her husband, meaning she was invariably nice to him." And on another occasion, "Somebody hit him on the head with a powerful telescope."

Fred Beck, of Los Angeles, has a many-sided mind, and one of its sides would suggest that he has the instincts of a promoter. He has written many notes in the night. One of his long memos concerned his belief that Catalina Island would make California's most beautiful residential suburb if it didn't have a water problem.

Mr. Beck, lying half asleep, decided he would subdivide the island and require that the purchaser of each lot donate a fifty-foot length of garden hose. All these hose lengths would be hooked together and coiled on a barge. The end would be attached to a faucet in the garden of Mr. Beck's brother-in-law, Nortie, in Santa Monica. The hose would then be unreeled from the barge, dramatically, in the manner of the Atlantic cable, and laid on the ocean floor; and thus would water be

21

brought to Catalina and an immense fortune to the pocket of Mr. Beck.

This same Fred Beck was once associated with the famous Farmers Market in Los Angeles. During that period he had a night thought which would bring a great flood of publicity for the market. He wrote it down, as follows: "Arrange have Capistrano swallows switch to F.M." Unhappily he didn't write down the part in which he had figured out how to do it — how to convince the swallows. He tells me that during the night he had it, he knew how it could be done, but that he was never able to remember it.

During the time when I was investigating the subject of night notes, a gentleman-adventurer named Desmond Slattery spent a week end at my house in the country. After he had gone back to the city I found some notes beside the bed he had used. I couldn't make any sense out of them. Here they are:

> Get Gov. underwrite my expenses go down
> state roundup — airlift — parachute 'em
> all over state.
> Important — issue statement to press
> denying this publicity stunt for song.

A few days later I saw Mr. Slattery again in New York and gave him his notes. He studied them awhile and then surprised me by remembering what they were about. He reminded me that the fire ants from Central America are swarming over the South, and especially over Alabama. Mr. Slattery proposed that he would go to Central America and stage an anteater roundup. Then he would organize an airlift and parachute anteaters all over the state of Alabama. As for the statement to the press, Mr. Slattery explained that he would issue it to deny that he was plugging a song titled "Anteaters Fell on Alabama."

A. J. Russell, one of the top writers in television, tells me that he once had a plotting problem, in connection with a TV-

22

drama script, that stayed with him for days and grew worse as time passed. He became irascible and mean, and kicked at flowers and spent hours pacing the floor. Finally came a morning when he was snarling his way through breakfast. Mrs. Russell tried to soothe him, telling him to be patient, that he'd get it solved in time; and then suddenly he leaped to his feet with a joyous cry. "I got it worked out last night," he shouted, "while I was half asleep! I wrote it down — the whole solution!" He raced to his bed table and snatched up a sheet of paper. There it was, in bold letters: "Quit the damn job."

Ann Maulsby, a writing neighbor of mine, has saved several brilliant examples of her own night notes. Once, she thought, in her twilight sleep, that she had found the perfect opening for a novel. She wrote it down sleepily and found the next day that it read:

> She was traveling around the world trying
> to learn how to be circular. She had never
> been circular.

Mrs. Maulsby has never written a novel to go on the end of that beginning, but I think she should. Also, I am an admirer of a poem she composed in the night. This time she couldn't even remember having written it down. She simply found the notes and recognized her own handwriting. Here it is:

> Stuck with the stuff of gardeners' dolls —
> One-half man and one-half woman.
> Little Mary Ott on her blot-stained cot,
> Plagued by austerer values than ours.

In my opinion it's as good as anything T. S. Eliot ever wrote.

Hugh Troy, who lives in Washington, D. C., is — in the Brooklyn phrase — a man of many facets, all turned on. Many lovely philosophical concepts come to him during the night. One of them turned up on his note pad as follows:

23

> Call State dept.
> All energy is state of mind. Going uphill
> is state of mind. Climb Everest — think
> downhill while climbing. You'll really be
> going downhill. Important.

I have been told about another Washington man, head of a powerful government agency, who evolved an elaborate Defense of Hatred one night and wrote it all down, believing that it might be so important that a new cabinet post would be needed to handle it. His notes, passed along to me, follow:

> Right to Hate is paramount, God-given
> To restrain hate is unhealthy. Don't bot-
> tle it up. Bring out in open. Market a
> Hate Kit. Little dolls like real people —
> Pres. Veep. Sens. Cabineters. Pins to
> stick in them. Candy dolls to be eaten.
> Slogan — EAT THE MAN YOU HATE.
> Slogan — HATE FOR HEALTH

I'm told that the citizen who inscribed those sentiments is one of the gentlest and kindest men in Washington.

Some years ago a writer came to me in Hollywood and showed me a scrawl on a piece of paper, which said, "The Sensitive Cucumber." He said he had written it down in the night, but he couldn't think what it meant and it had him worried. He wanted to know if I had ever heard him talking about cucumbers, sensitive or otherwise. I couldn't remember any such conversation. A week or so later I saw him again and asked him about it, and he said it had all been cleared up in another dream.

"Here I was," he said, "walking down a street, and suddenly right there on the sidewalk, in front of me, was a cucumber — a huge cucumber big around as a barrel, stretching across the sidewalk. I made a movement to the right, as if to go around

24

it, but it turned with me. I made a move in the other direction, and it turned with me — just like a radar scope. It was sensitive to every move I made, and I just couldn't get past it and had to turn around and go back home."

I told him I thought that "The Sensitive Cucumber" would make an excellent title for a book I was then writing, and asked him if I might have it, but he turned me down — said it was his dream and his cucumber and he'd write his own book to put it on. Real selfish.

Professor A. C. Knudson of Boston University used to tell his students a story about Ralph Waldo Emerson's habit of jotting down notes in the night. He kept a pad, a pencil, a candle, and matches beside his bed to make it just as handy as possible for him to record his magniloquent thoughts. In those days matches came in the form of a wafer-thin board with teeth. One night Emerson awoke, groped for the matches, broke off one, and tried to light it. No fire. He broke off another and tried it. Nothing. He kept at it until he had broken off all the matches and then, with unphilosophical chagrin, he went back to sleep without recording his sleepy-time thoughts. The next morning he was unable to recall those thoughts, and this upset him, but he was even more distressed when Mrs. Emerson said to him, "What has happened to my tortoise-shell comb? All the teeth are broken off."

There is, also, a story about Oliver Wendell Holmes the Elder. As a doctor he was interested in the use of ether as an anesthetic and once had a dose administered to himself. As he was going under, a great thought framed itself in his mind — he believed that he had grasped the key to all the mysteries of philosophy, a final solution to the central problem of existence. When he regained consciousness he was unable to think of it. But he had to recapture it, for it was of vital importance to mankind. He arranged to have himself given ether again and determined that he would speak the great thought

25

so that a stenographer could write it down. This time, just before the ether took full effect, he had the vision again, and he spoke the words and they were written down as follows:

> The entire universe is permeated with a
> strong odor of turpentine.

Earl Wilson tells about Leonard Stern, a television writer who always kept pad and pencil on his bedside table so that his thoughts in the night could be recorded. Stern trained himself to repeat, before going to sleep, this line: "Write it down. Write it down." One night he awoke and scribbled something on the pad and then went back to sleep. The next morning he found his notation: "Write it down."

I know a man, an architect-designer, who emerged from his nighttime coma with a great inspiration. He made a quick sketch on his pad, and in the morning found that he had designed a table with legs sticking straight out, like arms.

Ernie Rogers, the Atlanta newspaper columnist, tells me that he had a dream one night in which he fired a throng of fifty thousand to frenzied heights with the greatest oration ever delivered in the South, where eloquence is as rife as grits. At the conclusion of his speech, while the crowd went wild, Ernie woke up and scribbled the title of his speech so he would remember it in the morning. When he looked at it on arising he found these words: "Forsake Forsythe Forsooth." He says the only thing that makes sense about it is the word "Forsythe," which is the name of the county Atlanta is in, and even that doesn't make sense.

One of the weirdest perplexities to come out of this whole business of notes-in-the-night hit me one day when I found a scratch-pad in a dresser drawer with the following hieroglyphics in my own hand:

> Amaranth sasesusos Oronoco initiation secedes
> Uruguay Philadelphia.

I sat and looked at it a while and then said aloud, "Well, this is going a bit too far." I had a strong feeling that I was coming unstuck. I worried over those words for half a day and then dawn broke. I remembered. I hadn't written the words in the night. I had read them somewhere. The "Amaranth" sentence, if you can call it a sentence, is used by mechanics in typewriter factories when they make their final check-up on new machines. For reasons known only to God they bat out those words as a method of showing up any faulty alignment of the type bars. I had written them on the scratch-pad because I write all kinds of crazy things on scratch-pads. The thought suggests itself that a typewriter mechanic may be a more sensitive and more intelligent creature than we might suppose. Platitudinous prose is just as revolting to him as it ever was to Thomas Beer, an urbanely ironic author of the 1920's who, in the opinion of some literary historians, killed himself trying to produce a body of work without a single cliché in it. I can well imagine a mechanic becoming unhinged from constant typing about the season being auspicious for men of surpassing merit to perform some deed favorable to the political party of their choice.

Peggy McEvoy, whose late husband was the talented J. P., and who is herself a fine writer, tells me of a remarkable experience she had with a middle-of-the-night memo. She got up one morning, years ago, and discovered that she had set down some meaningless scrawls and then, in block letters, the following:

QUARK! A SERIES!

The words were there, but she could make no sense out of them, and neither could her husband, but they had a good laugh and then, as sometimes happens with these things, the phrase (if that's what it was) became a household saying. When either Peggy or J. P. came up with an idea for an article

27

or a series of articles or a book, and the idea was palpably silly, they would both cry out, often in unison, "Quark! A series!"

Long afterward Peggy was working on an article about Havana for *Life* and there was a brisk exchange of cables, as is the way with Lucelings. In the steady stream of messages from New York she noted, with a sort of extrasensory feeling, the continued use of the word "quark." Then one of the magazine's photographers arrived in Havana, and *he* began getting cables from home, and finally he said to Peggy, "What the hell is quark?" She had to confess she didn't know, but he, being a photographer and therefore more important than a writer, had enough nerve to ask New York, and New York replied that *quark* is cablese for question mark.

In conclusion I would like to offer two remarkable examples of night notes produced by Dale Eunson, a writer now resident in California. Once Mr. Eunson dreamed that he was a poet, reading his works to an audience in a vast amphitheater. His works consisted of one deathless line, and when he recited it, the enormous audience sat stunned, heads bowed in reverence, and then they arose as one man, shouting and screaming and clamoring to shake Mr. Eunson's hand, and lifting him to their shoulders for having at last revealed to them the Truth. When he awoke, Mr. Eunson hastily scribbled down the single line of his poem, so that the human race might benefit from it, and when he got around to reading it, this is what he found:

Oh, come see the deer, bighearted Oro

On another night Mr. Eunson was lying in bed, and it seemed to him that he was reading Louella Parsons' column in a newspaper. The column was in its customary position in the paper, but the type was large and flowery, as if illuminated by medieval monks, and the words were all in Gaelic. Mr. Eunson started to read the column and got through exactly four words before he woke up. He remembers that at the time he was enormously impressed by Miss Parsons' erudition, and he remembers writing down the four words. They were:

Whey shillic ick il.

Mr. Eunson says those words are graven forever on his memory, and sometimes in troubled moments he repeats them to himself. If it had happened to me, I'm sure I'd do the same.

5. THE LONGLIVITY OF LA LEGLONG

BACK IN THE ERA of Wonderful Nonsense there lived a young woman who was widely celebrated as the dumbest blonde on Broadway. Her name was Vera Milton, she worked for both Ziegfeld and Earl Carroll, and she was proud of the fact that the newspapers were constantly quoting her inane remarks.

I can remember two of her most famous utterances. She had been brought up in England and when a reporter asked her what she did for amusement over there, she replied airily, "Well, I spent a lot of time sliding down barristers." On another occasion she was riding through Central Park with a young man in a taxi. The young man had an arm draped around her shoulder and suddenly he said, "Miss Milton, you have marvelous potentialities." To which she responded, "Shhhh! The driver might hear you!"

Miss Milton was one of a long and fascinating line of women who are spiritual descendants of Mrs. Malaprop, the "old weather-beaten she-dragon" of Sheridan's play *The Rivals*. Mrs.

29

Malaprop was famous for her misapplication of words or, in her own phrase, her "nice derangement of epithets." She said that a certain person was "as headstrong as an allegory on the banks of the Nile," and she once remarked, "Lead the way and we'll precede."

Malapropisms have by no means disappeared from human speech. In fact, there are more of them now than ever before, because there are more people now than ever before. And it seems to me that they are funnier today than they were in the time of Mrs. Malaprop. To be perfectly truthful about it, I have never thought that Mrs. Malaprop was very good at committing malapropisms. Down through the years I have been hearing fresh and lively examples and whenever I hear them I write them down so I won't forget them. This practice dates back to my days as a young reporter in Denver, where my inspiration was the society editor of a Denver newspaper. She was a sweet and attractive girl, but she rarely let a day go by without creating some kind of fanciful and beautiful coinage. One day she wrote of how a local society leader had acquired "an expensive painting of Napoleon's son, La Leglong." And she once described a Denver family as being "famous for their longlivity."

Some of the finest malapropisms come from the lips of the uneducated, yet I've heard many splendid examples uttered by college graduates. The tradition is strong in my own family. I have a sister who once told me how she had seen "that Miller boy running down the street starch-naked." My daughter, when she was old enough to know better, acquired a "nit-nat shelf" and began collecting nit-nats for it (to this day all collections of trinkets and gimcracks are, to me, nit-nats). My wife has a remarkable facility for twisting sentences and misapplying words. She came out of a railroading family and one day when we were on the Super Chief, racing across the Arizona desert, she glanced out the window and said, "Well, he's certainly jackin' the ball." She once spoke of a man who had been lost at sea as having "gone to Casey Jones's locker." Recalling an old movie she had seen, she said that the boy hero "ran away and joined the French American Legion." I gave up trying to get her interested in baseball when I heard her refer to Warren Spahn as "a leftpaw."

Whenever Hysee comes to our house to help with the cleaning I can't resist eavesdropping on her conversations with my wife. Hysee (short for Hyacinth) talks a good deal about her husband. "He's olive-skinned," she says, "you know, sorta green." Reporting on the fact that he was on the water wagon, she said, "He's been unebriated for three months." She says that he spends a lot of time looking at television and that he prefers "stories about cow-bunchers." (I know a child who favors "defective stories" on TV.) Hysee also discusses the whims and vagaries of other women who employ her. Once I heard her say of a neighbor lady, "She acts as if butter wouldn't melt in her house." And of another, "She really laid it on with a towel."

I've heard Hysee tell of how she got so upset over a family crisis that "I drunk a whole bottle of nervous medicine." I've heard her, discussing plans for a small luncheon party, suggest, "You might start off with a plate of hot cuts." I've heard her describe a horror movie that was "enough to girdle your blood." But my favorite of all Hysee's sayings was spoken one day when I was driving her home. She said that her sister was bad sick and when I asked the nature of the trouble, she said, "She's got romantic author-itis." It struck me immediately that I have been trying to achieve the same condition for years.

Many of Hysee's expressions demonstrate that the unintentional garbling of words often produces more forceful and dynamic phrases and sentences than if the speaker employed impeccable English. Cow-bunchers, for example, seems to me to be a most apt way of describing the work performed by men on a cattle ranch. And I recall the time she said that a

31

certain person wasn't "the only peddler on the beach." That makes sense — I have seen some beaches where peddlers almost outnumbered the pebbles.

Harriet Van Horne, the New York television critic, finds great virtue in the malapropisms committed by one of her friends. "Her slips of the tongue," says Miss Van Horne, "are never the banal kind; they're lit from within, and they strike home like pin-point bombing. Conventional language pales by comparison."

Miss Van Horne's friend speaks of a shy, withdrawn young man as "a very self-erasing person." She is critical of television comedians for "always telling those same old Joe Morris jokes." And of one particular comedy show she says, "It's getting honkier and tonkier." A lovely phrase, fit to stand beside the more famous Goldwynism: "I want a picture that is blood and thirsty."

An editor friend of mind in New York remembers a lady who, in discussing a new dress, said, "It fits like a fiddle." He has heard another lady employ the expression, "It pries on my mind," and still another who said, "I got it straight from the horse's hoof."

Charlotte Montgomery knows a woman who is quite skillful at mangling syntax. "There are people," she has said, "who never work hard unless someone is plodding them from behind." This same woman, describing her condition of weariness, said, "I'm worn to a fragile." On another occasion she described a man as having "gone to sea as a stoleaway," and once she coined a lovely word in the sentence "She wrote me a letter that gave me an inkle that something like this might happen." I suppose an inkle is a very small inkling.

Among my neighbors is a lady whose conversation always enchants me because she deals almost exclusively in gossip and because she is always trying to use high-flown language. Once she was discussing the custom of common-law marriage. "It

32

has existed," she said, "from time in a memorial." Of another neighbor: "She's got a bean in her bonnet." Expressing her opinion of a certain political candidate, she concluded, "Nobody will vote for him but the hoi polio." And once I heard her speak scornfully to her husband: "Are you a man or a moose?"

Not long ago, while preparing for a trip to Mexico, I met a young woman who had spent some time traveling in that country. She began describing her own adventures and finally said, "And while I was in San Miguel the Indians put on a wonderful fiasco." This same young woman had a peculiar way of transposing words and sounds. Two or three times she said, for emphasis, "Believe me you!" And when I sought information about the dangers of tourist sickness, she said, "Really, you're making a mountain out of a mill hole."

That last example is not technically a malapropism, but a spoonerism, and spoonerisms occupy a special place in the world of grammatical confusion. I would like to cite two specimens that have been contrived in my presence and which seem to border on the classical. One evening a lady was visiting in my home and she wanted to remind us that we were all going to the opening performance of *The Caine Mutiny Court Martial* in New York. "Don't forget now," she said, "we're going to *The Taine Courtney Moot Martial.*" It was a spoonerism of rare beauty, ranking with André Baruch's celebrated program opening of years ago: "Good ladies, evening and gentlemen of the audio radiance." I was afraid I would forget the sequence of sounds in *The Taine Courtney Moot Martial* so I grabbed a pencil and wrote it down the moment I heard it. It became so firmly embedded in my mind that I still have difficulty speaking the correct title of the play, even when I'm talking to Herman Wouk, its author.

Another spoonerism of excellent quality was spoken to me recently by a hotel manager. I must confess that he had just consumed two martinis (tee martoonis) and he was telling me about some of the important people who had been guests in his hotel of late. "And then," he said, "just last week we had the actor, Razzle Bath-bone."

Let's not assume that either the malapropism or the spoonerism belongs exclusively to the women, even though they seem to be more prone to garble than the men. I have heard some good ones uttered by members of my own sex. There is, for example, a prominent contractor in our town who speaks of certain people as being "mechanically clined." And I once heard him describe a carpenter as having "a pediment in his speech." I bled for the poor man, because a pediment is a low triangular gable crowned with a projecting cornice. I might also mention the delivery man who once said of a friend, "He wears bi-follicle eyeglasses." And on another occasion, describing a dance he had attended, he said that "the party got real roarious."

Still, it takes a woman to perform true wonders with words and even names. I have heard about a first-grade teacher who, on the first day of school had each pupil stand and give his or her name. A little boy got up and said his name was Gooey Miller. The teacher thought it an unusual Christian name, and that afternoon, when Gooey's mother came to get him, they had a conversation.

"Is your boy's name really Gooey?" the teacher asked.

"Yes," said the mother.

"How did you happen to give him that name?"

"I read it in a book."

"How do you spell it?" the teacher wanted to know.

"G-u-y, Gooey," obliged the mother.

Another story tells of an elderly lady in Alabama who was visited by the census taker. When he asked for her first name, she replied, "Pishie."

"Would you spell it for me?" he asked.

"Don't rightly know how to spell it," she said, "but I got a calendar here where it's spelled out."

She brought out the calendar, which featured a color picture of Cupid's girl friend, Psyche.

Well, it *could* be Pishie.

꽃꽃꽃꽃꽃꽃꽃꽃꽃꽃꽃꽃꽃꽃꽃꽃꽃꽃꽃꽃꽃꽃

6. THE COWPIKE AFFAIR

YEARS AGO the publicity director of Paramount Pictures in Hollywood was a man named George Brown. Mr. Brown was both amiable and shrewd. He was a man who had fought his way to the top without benefit of formal education. Most so-called self-made men who never made it through the elementary grades are inclined to be contemptuous of college-bred people, but George Brown took the opposite view — he had enormous respect for anybody with a solid university background.

One day a young man named Bernie Kamins applied for a job at Paramount and after he identified himself as a recent graduate of Harvard, Mr. Brown unhesitatingly put him to work. One of Mr. Brown's chief assistants assigned Mr. Kamins to the job of publicizing westerns. Mr. Kamins knew nothing whatever about cowboy pictures or cowboy literature, but he set to work with a will. He went into the files to find out how other people had handled their publicity matter on westerns. In one of these mimeographed releases Mr. Kamins came upon the word "cowpike." It was a typographical mistake and should have been cowpoke, but Mr. Kamins didn't know that and so, when he started writing his own copy on

35

current horse operas, he frequently referred to cowboys as cowpikes.

Now it happens that Mr. Kamins' immediate boss was a fellow who didn't like college men, and especially Harvard men, and so instead of correcting Mr. Kamins, he went to George Brown and complained.

"That new guy Kamins," he said, "is a real jerkenheimer. He can't even spell. He insists on calling cowboys cowpikes."

"So, what *should* he call them?" demanded Mr. Brown.

"Why, cow*pokes,* of course."

"Listen, Gene," said Mr. Brown, "let's get one thing straight right now. That boy is a graduate of Harvard. If he says it's cowpike then, god damn it, it's cowpike."

And cowpike it was for the duration of Mr. Kamins' employment at Paramount.

7. THE MARVELOUS LANGUAGE OF SPORTS

A DOZEN YEARS ago a part-time lexicographer named Parke Cummings published a fat volume called *The Dictionary of Sports,* in which some nine thousand words and phrases associated with every known sporting activity, from stabbing bulls to shooting pool, were defined. It is my intention to launch an oblique criticism against the book, though I must concede its value in certain directions. But for Mr. Cummings' dictionary I would probably go to my urn without ever knowing the nature of a *fliffus.* A *fliffus* is a trapeze trick adapted to the sport of tumbling. I am happy to know about a *fliffus* though I have no desire to fliff.

In addition to all the more common terms, Mr. Cummings lexicogs a good many recondite sporting words. A *hobber,* as meaning a leaner in horseshoes or quoits, is recondite to me. A *googly* is a ball, in cricket, thrown with a special kind of spin on it, while a *gogsee* is a tee used in curling. A *prad* is another name for a horse, and when a prad gets the *wobbles* he is suffering from a nervous ailment. An *anyhow* is a kind of lift used by weight-lifters, and a *leaping powder* is a stiff drink taken by a fox hunter just before the hunt begins.

Let it be admitted that Mr. Cummings has done the job he set himself to do, and that he has done it well. I contend, however, that the language of sports in America, in its most colorful aspect, cannot be found in his dictionary. I looked in vain, for instance, for the word *trut.* It belongs on page 475, between *trunks* and *try.* It was admitted (or thrust) into the language of sports in 1948 by Rocky Graziano, currently devoting his talents to dramaturgy. In that year Mr. Graziano lost his middleweight boxing title to Tony Zale in Chicago. When the fallen champ returned to New York someone asked him what he thought of the people of Chicago. "They trut me good," he said. Ever since hearing it I have regarded the old-fashioned words "treat" and "treated" as being pallid and flabby. Even today, in the 1960's, I find myself saying such things as, "I'm a grown man and I want to be trut as one." And at Halloween time I think in terms of "trick or trut."

Sports writers of the 1930's and earlier would never have quoted Rocky Graziano as saying, "They trut me good." The quote would likely have appeared in the newspapers as, "They treated me wonderfully," or, "The good people of Chicago were extraordinarily considerate and I am grateful to them."

The present-day effort of sports writers to quote their people with unswerving accuracy is the greatest technical advance the trade has witnessed in its whole history. When Joe Jacobs delivered himself of the immortal phrase "We wuz

37

robbed," I have an idea that a majority of the sports writers went back to their shops and wrote it, "My fighter was cheated." When the same Joe Jacobs cried in anguish, "I should of stood in bed," most of the newspaper boys probably translated it to something like, "If I had known things were going to develop in this fashion, I doubt if I would have left home this morning."

In partial support of the foregoing, I would like to recall an experience I had back in the 1930's during one of the recurring Golden Eras of American Sports. I attended most of the leading sports events as a reporter assigned to do the "color" story. On the night that Max Baer knocked out Primo Carnera at Madison Square Garden Bowl I was in Carnera's dressing room immediately after the fight ended. Half a dozen sports writers were there too. The seconds brought the felled ox in, holding him by both arms because he had the stumbles. He was truly a sight to behold.

Gaffers of my bracket may remember that Mr. Baer struck Mr. Carnera with great force and great frequency about the face and head. When the Italian giant reached the dressing room he had large lumps all over his forehead, and his jaws were swollen. They took his ring clothes off and propped him up on a rubbing table, and he began looking around the room without apparently seeing anything. His handlers faded back and left him sitting there. Nobody made a move to do anything, so I stepped up to him.

"Did he hit you hard?" I asked him.

He stared at me for a full minute. Then his lips moved.

"Holy Jesus!" he said.

"Do you want to fight him again?"

"Holy Jesus!" mumbled Carnera.

"Do you think you could lick him if you fought him again?"

"Holy Jesus!"

"Does your head hurt?"

38

"Holy Jesus!"

"Do you think Baer can lick Schmeling?"

"Holy Jesus!"

At this point half a dozen or so of Carnera's proprietors (he was owned in toto and in fee simple) came crashing in and the press was ordered out of the place. I was well satisfied. It was one of the most revealing interviews I had ever had. I was quite astonished, however, the next day when I picked up the papers to see what the sports writers had to say about that scene in the dressing room. One of them quoted Carnera as having said:

"Max's blows were very hard. He hurt me several times — I'll have to admit that. But I sincerely believe that I could defeat him and I would like to have another chance. I want to regain the championship."

Carnera couldn't have uttered those thirty-eight words in that sequence if he had gone four years to Harvard. Yet the other sports writers had quoted him the same way, with variations in the actual language.*

Today the sports writers have attuned themselves to the vagrant, magic phrase, and when it comes, they grab hold of it and take joy in it and put it in the paper the way it was uttered. This, however, will not last. The pressure continues for the standardization of all speech. We of the writing trade risk persecution and perhaps even physical danger if we are accurate in quoting a Negro who speaks with a Southern dialect and drawl. (Thus far it is all right for us to quote a white person's Southern dialect and drawl, but that too will be forbidden in the end.) We risk public condemnation and embarrassment if we are ac-

* I must admit that I was unable to quote Carnera accurately in my own account of the interview. I doubt that even today the newspapers would let "Holy Jesus!" get by. But I, at least, reported that the Italian was unable to answer questions intelligibly. A few years later I was able to publish a true account in a book, _Low Man on a Totem Pole_. A book is almost the only medium through which a writer can speak his mind nowadays.

curate in quoting a person who speaks with a Jewish accent. The Irish are beginning to holler against writers who quote their true Irish brogue — they want their talk to be recorded as if it came from the lips of Winston Churchill. The Italians will soon be threatening those of us who fancy ourselves as skillful in setting down their colorful way with English; the many Italian comedians and singers can get away with it on the stage and on television, but when non-Italians have a try at it, they are likely to hear rumblings of discontent.

Laws-a-mussy! Bagging podden, pliz. Begorra and Oi've shtrayed a farrr distance from me subject! Skoosa!

A compilation of famous sports phrases would not need to be 100 per cent slang. Slang words would bulk large in it, for sports is replete with them — words fully as splendid as the *jista* of the barber trade; a *jista,* in the jargon of barbers, is a customer regarded with slight disfavor because all he wants is jista shave. (This reminds me of some friends who operate an antique shop, and who speak unhappily of be-backers — people who come in and browse and buy nothing and then say they'll be-back.)

On the other hand, the name of the late Philadelphia Jack O'Brien would appear in such a compilation because of his ability to utter magniloquent sentiments in which he managed a delicate fusing of slang and bombast. His technique is evident in the remark he made after Stan Ketchel knocked him bow-legged. Said O'Brien: "I had heard of his tumultuous ferocity but conjectured that I would jab his puss off." Another fine example of O'Brien's eloquence: "I should of put the bum away early but my timing was a fraction of an iota off."

Much has been made of the atrocities committed by Dizzy Dean in the time that he has been a radio and TV broadcaster. School authorities have, from time to time, complained against Diz's mangling of the language as a bad example to the kiddies. They have spoken out against his employment of such expressions as "He slood into second," and "He swang at a third strike." These dizzydeanisms belong in our compendium even though the struggle with preterits is not alone confined to the world of sports; these locutions are almost as common as the double negative in the language of the people. A fine example, as reported by Horace Reynolds, came from the lips of a Tennessee hill dweller who had driven past a friend on the highway without speaking. Charged with this oversight, the hillbilly apologized, saying, "If I'd a knowed it was you I'd of retch out and wove."

Dizzy Dean's true glory, in any book of famous sayings in sports, would likely stem from certain of his utterances during his pitching days. Among the best, I think, was a question he asked during the celebrated World Series of 1934, when Dizzy and the Cardinals beat Detroit. In the ninth inning of the final and deciding game, Dean stood on the mound and saw the great Hank Greenberg come to the plate, wagging a big bat. Dizzy gazed at Greenberg with more than a little contempt, and then spoke loudly and clearly. "What's the matter?" he called out. "Ain't you people got no peench hitters?" Following which he proceeded to strike out Detroit's star batsman.

Dean might prove to be the chief contributor to a book of quotations from the world of sports, for there is a cockeyed quality to his casual remarks, on and off the field, that has led many of us to believe that he is not altogether real — that he is a fictional creature out of the pages of Ring Lardner. A bit later I'll give you an account of Dizzy's highly original method of describing the actual play in baseball.

Always defiant of authority as well as precedent, he has frequently come close to proving himself right when he was clearly wrong. In driving an automobile, for example, he recognizes no rule as affecting himself, and once a policeman stopped him as he came ripping through a one-way street, traveling of course in the forbidden direction.

"You blind?" demanded the policeman. "Didn't you see them erras, said this is a one-way street?"

"Sure I seen 'em," said Diz. "How many ways you think I'm a-goin'?"

The late Charlie Moran, umpire in the National League, belongs in our collection for having once made a statement which clearly lifts umpiring into the realm of creative art. A dispute arose over a certain play and Moran hesitated before pronouncing judgment. One of the players demanded, "Well, is it safe, or is it a out?" Whereupon Charlie Moran issued his historic pronunciamento: "It ain't *nothing* till I call it."

The "good field, no hit" of Mike Gonzales belongs in our book, if for no other reason than that it is quoted so often, and so does the brilliant coinage *usen't*. This word was picked out of the language of baseball players by the comedian Phil Silvers, a devout follower of the game, and Mr. Silvers uses it in his comedy routines. It is employed in baseball in this fashion: "Usen't you used to be with Philly?"

There's a line, too, from the sayings of the great Rube Waddell which deserves preservation. When he made his first appearance as a major-league pitcher, one of the batters hit the ball back to the mound. Rube scooped it up, took careful aim, and fired it at the batter who was running toward first base. The ball struck the runner and all but killed him, and there was an immediate uproar directed against the country boy on the mound. But the Rube was not intimidated and amid all the tumult he issued a solemn announcement: "Listen, whirr I come frum, that's a out."

The contributions of Red Barber, the broadcaster who was once called The Verse of Brooklyn in the years he spent with the Dodgers, should not be overlooked. In his colorful Brooklyn phase Mr. Barber performed the all but impossible feat of corrupting the most corrupt language on earth; he implanted hog-and-hominy talk into the vernacular of the Brooklyn baseball fan. Many figures of speech belonging to the Deep South are in common usage today among the former-faithful of Flatbush, even though their ball team has gone away. Among them are "eatin' high off the hawg," "sittin in th' catbird seat," "swarmin' like flies around a barrel of sorghum," "tearin' up the pea patch," "heavier than a bucket of hawg livers," and "slippery as a plate of boiled okra." Mr. Barber's frequent use of the exclamatory "Oh, Doctah!" is common nowadays up and down Bedford Avenue and can be heard in season along the crowded sands of Coney. And he has given the phrases "meat hand" and "tools of ignorance" wide currency. The ungloved hand of a player is called his meat hand, as in "It hit him on his meat hand." Ballplayers refer to a catcher's equipment as the "tools of ignorance," meaning that the catcher's job is so hazardous and so filled with contusions and abrasions and fractures that only an ignorant fellow would accept it.

Let us not overlook the magnificent two-word comment of a Dodger fanatic who, at mention of the name of the hated Giants, exploded: "Them scum!" And the complimentary phrase, "He won't rub" — another redbarberism. This is said of a player who has just been hit by a pitched ball. As he makes his way down to first base the eyes of the other ballplayers are on him, and the eyes of the fans, and the observation is made, "He won't rub." Meaning that he is too much of a masculine man to even touch the aching, burning spot where the ball struck him. If he *does* rub, they get ready to bring out the stretcher.

There is, of course, no end to the number of words and phrases that need to be put into a formal record and preserved for future generations. I think of Tommy Loughran, the ex-fighter who turned radio announcer for a while and one evening said, "It won't take the referee long before I think he should stop it." And somewhere in the writings of John Lardner there is a quotation concerning the football team at Centre

College in Kentucky, in an era long departed — the team known as the Praying Colonels from the widely publicized fact that its members paused for prayer in moments of dire emergency. The quotation came from the lips of the Centre coach, presumably during a half-time session in the dressing room. It goes: "Down on your knees, boys, here comes Grantland Rice!"

According to Murray Robinson, a Brooklyn pitcher of yesteryear named Leo Dickerman was the true author of one of baseball's immortal utterances, often attributed to others. On a day when Dickerman believed that his teammates had let him down through the commission of a series of fielding errors, he foreswore any further team-play cooperation on his part, crying out in anger: "From now on it's every man for theirself."

Managers of the stripe of Casey Stengel and Leo Durocher and Charlie Dressen have made abundant contributions to the glossary of rounders. Dressen belongs if only for his creation, "The Giants is dead." (Later, when Dressen was bounced as Dodger manager, a New York newspaper reported the news under a headline, DRESSEN ARE DEAD.)

Among the inspirational quotations worthy of consideration is one by Roy Campanella, the former Dodger catcher. Someone was speaking to him about his agility in backing up both first and third. Said Roy: "Any place I can git that nobody else has gotten, I git."

It should be evident by now that the sports world is teeming with people who are masters of the English language. They are masters of it in the sense that they are superior to it. They employ it in the classic manner of a Chaucer or a Ring Lardner, wrenching it into lovely distortions, committing unbelievably beautiful crimes in the realm of syntax, often manufacturing their own glorious words as they go along. One of my favorite reference books is Bartlett's Familiar Quotations. I use it constantly in my work, and to settle nasty arguments in the living

44

room, and yet I am unhappy with it for the reason that the only sports character I've been able to find in its 1500 pages is Joe Jacobs, whose most famous remarks are mentioned above. All the old reliables are in Bartlett, such things as damn the torpedoes, and what this country needs, and git thar fustest with the mostest, and give me liberty, and war is hell, and don't swap horses, and so on. Yet the editors have all but ignored an area in which the English-American language has been given its most colorful and exciting employment.

I have saved four prize items for the last.

In the spring of 1949 Vince Foster, a boy from Nebraska who was almost universally regarded as a coming champion, entered the prize ring against Charlie Fusari. Mr. Fusari knocked Mr. Foster down in the first round. Then he knocked him down again, and again after that, and then a fourth time. The referee concluded that Mr. Fusari had shown himself to be the superior fighter, and led the battered and bewildered Mr. Foster to a chair. A bit later in the dressing room the reporters arrived for the purpose of obtaining the viewpoint of the vanquished fighter. All that Mr. Foster had to say to them was this:

"I wisht they had of let it went."

I have heard that there is a sports orator in Boston named Swede Nelson and I would enjoy meeting him for two reasons. I would like to know what a sports orator does when he is being one, and I admire a thing Mr. Nelson is reported to have cried out, presumably in a majestic oratorical flourish, to wit: "The greatest football player in America hasn't been born yet!"

The loveliest and most quotable line to come out of tennis was passed along to me by J. Bryan, III, who got it from a man who was baseline umpire in a championship match in which Adrian Quist, the Australian; was competing. The umpire was standing near Quist and watched him miss three shots in a row. At this point the Australian let his racquet drop to the ground, seized his head in his hands, and cried out in down-under anguish:

"Eyedrian, Eyedrian, wye do you plye this gyme!"

Several years ago during the closing weeks of a hot pennant race in the American League, Cleveland came into the Yankee Stadium carrying a slight edge in the standings. Just before the start of one of the games Red Barber took his microphone and TV camera to the Cleveland dugout and interviewed a few of the players. I was at home, watching, when Red asked Larry Doby how he thought the day's game might end. The big fellow shrugged and said: "I just woosh we were a little far aheader."

Which reminds me of a more recent sentence uttered by the talented actress, Shelley Winters. Said Miss Winters:

"Maybe I do have buck teeth, but I know a few stars who have bucker."

---

8. DIZ AT THE MIKE

IN THE baseball season of 1950, Dizzy Dean was brought in to New York as television announcer for the Yankees. Within a week after he had started his new job the statistical purists, known as Figger Filberts, were complaining. They took no amusement whatever out of Dizzy's unorthodox performance at the microphone. They were furious when, on occasion, Diz would suddenly forget the ball game altogether and break into a song about goin' fishin' in th' crawdad hole. To statistical fans baseball is a dead-serious business. There's no room in it for laughter and frivolity. If a cat comes scampering onto the playing field and eludes capture for ten minutes, holding up the progress of the game, they are indignant about it, and cuss the cat and cuss the rest of us who whoop and cheer and howl with laughter.

Dizzy Dean represented, then, a new and delightful diversion for me, and for people like me; the things he did and the things he said were often as entertaining as the ball games he was describing, or neglecting to describe. Much of the stuff that has been written about his slang and his dialect and his own private grammar has missed the mark. The sports writers can't decide whether he says a man slood into second, or slud. Someone once tried to write an account of Dizzy's appearance on a television panel show, and missed the boat altogether. Dizzy was seated next to H. V. Kaltenborn during that program, and Mr. Kaltenborn needled him gently about his abuse of the English language. The newspaper critic wrote that Diz gave answer, addressing the dean of American newscasters as "Mister Kaltenbrown." It happens that I was listening to the show and wrote down what Diz said, as follows: "Well, now, I tell ya, Mister Kattlinbomb, it's this way . . ."

There are, as mentioned earlier, many do-gooders who would like to see Dizzy barred from channels of public communication on the grounds that he is exercising a deleterious influence on the hordes of children who listen to his Ozarkian rhetoric. These complainants say that if it isn't stopped, the children will begin talking the way Dizzy talks. Well, suppose they do. It's talkin', ain't it?

During that 1950 season I watched most of the Yankee home games with pad and pencil beside me, and recorded many of the peculiar Dean locutions. At that time Ira Smith and I were working on the second of two books loaded with humorous stories out of the world of baseball (*Low and Inside* and *Three Men on Third*). At the end of the season I recorded my Dizzy Dean notes on Eaton's Berkshire Eminence Bond and we had a brisk opening for our book.

47

Diz has certain speech mannerisms which recur frequently in his haphazard narration of a ball game. A player thew a ball or thode it. An umpire is an umparr. Everybody on the playing field does everything nonchalantly. That is his favorite big word. "There he goes," says Diz, "walkin' nonchalantly up to the plate." He spoke once of a passed batter "trottin' nonchalantly down to first," and remarked that it was dern funny that a player walked but he didn't actual walk but trotted. He described another player as "squattin' nonchalantly in the on-deck circle." Once when a batter had fanned, Dizzy described him as "walkin' nonchalantly back to the dugout in diss-gust." The TV screen one day was holding a close-up of home plate while Catcher Yogi Berra was out at the mound conferring with his pitcher. As Berra started back to his position his feet and then his legs came into view at the top of the television screen. Said Diz: "There comes Berra's shin guards walkin' nonchalantly back to the plate." And again, "That tremenjous roar you hear is Ted Williams walkin' nonchalantly up to the batter's box."

Sometimes a batter "walks disgustilly" back to the dugout after fanning. Sometimes he "stands confidentially" at the plate. And the players come off the "bainch" to "take their respectable positions."

A ball is "farred over to second" and a third strike sometimes "retarrs the side." When a pitcher fields a bunt, Diz says, "He bounced on it like a cat on a mouse." A hard-hit ground ball that gets away from an infielder is usually described as having "karmed off his glove."

Dizzy speaks of "sprang training" and "peench hitters" and the relief pitcher "thowin' down his plimminary pitches." He summarizes: "No hits, no runs, no airs." Errors are always airs. He describes conferences "in the middle of the diament." He says time has been called while a base runner "is lacening up his shoestrings." He becomes the baseball oracle when he re-

marks, "They's gonna be a little fancy stragedy pulled off now."
The adverb "far" is always "for" in the Dean lexicon. "Lopat's
got five strike-outs in the ball game so for," he says. Or, "As
you seen on your screen, that's the first air of the ball game so
for." He described a hard-laboring pitcher as having "puss-
peration clean thew his uniform." And in announcing a pamphlet which the public may get by writing in, he says, "You can
have the new Yankee sketch book if you woosh."

During a close shot of a batter, Dizzy advises: "Look careful
now and you can see the heesive tape on his neck." Once
when Joe DiMaggio made a magnificent catch deep in center
— running with his back toward the plate and reaching high
above his head to snag a fly ball, Dizzy yelled: "Holy cow! He
caught it with his back in front of the pitcher's box!"

In a preseason exhibition game at the stadium, Dizzy uttered
the following remarkable sentence: "That loads the Brooklyn
Dodgers fulla bases." Speaking once of a player coming up to
bat, he said, "He resembles Crosetti like he used to look." And
on the occasion of a spirited rhubarb, he remarked, "They
better watch out. That umparr used to be an ex-fighter." He is
usually contrite when he makes a mistake in calling a play. "I
bag your pardon, folks," he says, "I'm ignernt."

"This is what you call a real slugger's fest," he explained one
day. And for the benefit of amateur scorekeepers: "You gotta
give the pitcher a sist on that." Discussing Ted Williams admiringly, he said: "Look at that stance on 'im! Brother, they's
rhythm in that stance!" And of the Red Sox catcher: "Most all
ballplayers got nicknames and Birdie Tebbetts's is Birdie because he's always ahollerin' like a little ole kinairy bird." Recalling the career of Dolph Camilli, he said: "There was one of
the gracefulest first basemans I ever seen." And during a tight
situation in a close game, he remarked, "Brother, they's a
lotta nerverackin' out there on that field right now." Dizzy's
comment on the lazily relaxed manner of Joe Gordon was:

"Look at 'im. There's a fella you look at 'im you say, there's a fella dreads to do *anything*."

Sometimes Dizzy tries to be helpful to his audience, explaining things about baseball itself or about his own linguistic obfuscations. He spoke once of the futility of quarreling with an umpire, saying, "You might as well try to argy with a stump." After a moment's reflection, he continued: "Some of you New York folks might not know what a stump is. Well, I'll tell ya. A stump is a wood thing . . . well, it's somethin' a tree has been cut down off of."

One day when a visiting manager was making his way to the mound for the purpose of yanking his pitcher, Dizzy filled in with information out of his own vast experience.

"You folks," he said, "prob'ly wonder what's goin' on out there — what they're sayin' to one another. Well, I had some experience pitchin' and I can tell you what's goin' on. In the first place, that pitcher he's hot as a farrcracker. And he prob'ly don't like the idee of bein' took out. So when the manager comes walkin' nonchalantly out to the mound, the pitcher he says, 'Aw, fer cryin' out loud!' So the manager he says, 'Now take it easy, son. You cain't win *ever'* day.' So the pitcher he says, 'Aw, fer cryin' out loud! If I coulda got that one guy out, that bum, they never woulda got nowheres offa me.' Then the manager he says, 'Now take it easy, son. You go on and take a sharr and git some rest and maybe you can beat 'em tuhmarr.' So the pitcher's purty burned up, and he says, 'Aw, fer cryin' out loud!' But he's gotta go, so he goes. That's approximate-ly what goes on out there at the mound, folks."

At times he becomes a philosopher, as in his salute to Phil Rizzuto when the Yankee shortstop insisted on staying in the game after being hurt. "Brother," exclaimed Diz, "I wanna tell you that's dee-termination and will parr to play baseball!"

One day at stretch time in the seventh, he remarked, "Well, the fans has all stood up and woosht the Yankees good luck."

50

Approaching the plate, a batter bent over to get some dirt on his hands, eliciting from Dizzy the following observation: "I want you folks to take a good look at that. Lookit him rubbin' his hands around in the dirt. I 'member when I was a little kid and useta go out and play in the dirt and then when we'd go home arr mothers would whip us. Well, sir, right there in fronta your eyes is big grown men out there playin' in the dirt. Doggone if this ain't a crazy world!"

The camera, which Dizzy always calls "the camery," moved up close to an umpire standing near second base one afternoon.

"Lookit that umparr," said Diz, "standin' out there with his arms behind his back. Umparrs don't never seem to know what to do with their hands. They cither got them behind their backs or folded. Lookit 'im out there! Looks sorta like a statcha."

Dizzy complains frequently about the amount of written material that is handed him in the course of a game because he has to read it and he doesn't like to read. After struggling through a long written commercial one afternoon he concluded with: "Well, at least I got through to the end. I admit I cain't read good. But they's one thing I know. When that pitcher thows that ball, he thows it. When that ketcher ketches it, he ketches it. An' when that hitter hits it, he hits it. That's all you gotta know, folks."

9. *OF* VARIETY *AND ABEL*

ONE OF the most fecund creators of new words and phrases in the American language is the theatrical trade paper *Variety,* often called the Bible of Show Biz. H. L. Mencken, author of the monumental three-volume study *The American Language,* paid frequent and glowing tribute to *Variety*'s contributions, and called the publication's staff "advance agents of change in American slang." George Bernard Shaw once said, "I thought I knew the English language until one day I picked up *Variety*." He was so fascinated by the paper's lingo, which he could not understand, that he became an immediate subscriber. The *Saturday Review* once said that *Variety* "has influenced the American language more than any other periodical." And Jules Archer, in a magazine article, described its style as "a polyglot of slang, abbreviation, Esperanto, shorthand, smart Alec metaphor, dialect, patois, macaronics, and super-Biblical brevity."

I have been an admirer and a customer of *Variety* for many years, and consider it to be the best trade publication I've ever seen. I cherish the friendship of its editor, Abel Green, a dynamic guy who actually talks in *Varietyese*.

Once I undertook, just for the fun of it, to review a literary classic in the prose style of *Variety*. I showed it to Mr. Green and he snatched it away from me and published it in the anniversary edition of his paper. On rereading it I find that much of it would make no sense at all to people who are not acquainted with *Variety*, so I have appended a glossary plus a few explanatory notes. So, here is:

"ALICE" IN JIVE

Book attracting beaucoup comment around N. Y. tagged "Alice in Wonderland." Tome snagging terrif bally despite fact it's channeled at juve trade. Among nip-ups noted is one by Alec Woollcott, pastured crick. Intro is by Woollcott. Info Please mob upping interest in story via rave quotes from text. Retail store check reveals pop price not luring kiddies from current yen for prose of torso-tossers and fanners. Steady sale of book confined to uppercase nondraftables.

"Variety" cuffo-mugg caught tale in reprint edition with Woollcott blurb. Author hancocks self Lewis Carroll but understood he's really English Rev. named Dodgson. Illustrations by John Tenniel nsg, considerably below par set by prehistoric cartoonists who etched principals in Thaw trial.

Author making obvious pitch for Coast cash. Story apparently started as script for Disney tinter. Meller getaway soon dwindles to dull slapstick. Femme lead lacks s. a. needed for b. o. if pix go for this one. Tale opens with grade-school siren at leisure on stuff called grass. Minx is obviously on dimwit side and half asleep in first sentence. Has insane hair follicles. Action opens when talking rabbit enters. Author not satisfied to have gabby hare, but has Easter-egger lugging a watch.

Perils-of-Pauline gimmick has doll pratfall into deep well searching for animated hassenpfeffer. Arrives at spot resembling Hialeah infield to find flagon tagged "Drink Me." Stuff's apparently dynamite and subdeb discovers self preshrunk. Throughout scenario she's continually shriveling or adding poundage. Author angles for wet hanky trade with femme bawling constantly, once yowling a puddle of eyewash that nearly drowns her.

Doll finally locates looney rabbit and gets her claws on a fan that belongs to him. Big chance to hypo story here but author's clerical background apparently damp-blanketed any sallyrandification. Clearly a clerical error.

Gal's routine slides through meetings with mob of Disney type characters and she has such a groggy noggin she thinks she's dame named Mabel, also a dopess. Encounters mouse and tries to sell him a bill of goods on a puss named Dinah (possibly a role for Fanny Rose Shore?). Animal gab is strictly hokey throughout. Hayfield sequence finds heroine snagging leaf from a thing called a buttercup and for a moment reader feels the w. k. terp turn is about to begin but siren doesn't even shed her rayons. No peeling for this babe.

Daffy characters include King and Queen, assorted gremlins and leprechauns and menehunes and quite a few tarts. Author shamelessly fobs off oldies in the yock dept., including the feeble gag about Cheshire Cat grinners, plus such whiskered clichés as "curiouser and curiouser" and "old Father William." Tried to needle action with pot-throwing sequence, but Abbott & Costello scripters do better. Introduces drunken turtle who spews puns faster than Cerf, and wastes chapter on al fresco brawl involving another rabbit and a daft hat mfr. Sequence is a direct theft from "The Man Who C T D," though in present instance the dialogue smells. Au-

53

thor's effort here was to create psycho ward situash but idea brodies and merely resembles table talk at Lindy's.

Climax spotlights screwy croquet game (oke fodder for Woollcott, a wicket man) followed by shabby device of jury trial done à la Cliff Nazarro with all hands orry-eyed.

Understand Disney unlikely to option yarn despite nods it's getting via literati and caviar mob. Story ed at major studio, a Rhodes scholar, reported interested. Intro describes author as celibate, hence his scorn for s. a. motif. Suggestion is he'd object to fleshy musical production. Tentful of animals involved in story but even they've been paulmossed — frogs and fishes and rabbits costumed more elaborately than Menjou. Juve siren's gams never once mentioned.

Mess might be succored for pix as nabe house throw-in. Script needs Ben Hecht to unsapolio story, handing femme lead to Ava Gardner or Linda Christian and subbing Sinatra for rabbit. Cole Porter score would help particularly in sequences involving tarts.

Understood author already plotting sequel involving tragic character, fat slob labeled Humpty Dumpty. Has Laughton in mind.

A SORT OF GLOSSARY

Bally — ballyhoo, publicity.

Juve — pertaining to jerkenheimers in their teens.

Crick — critic.

Torso-tossers — strip-tease artists.

Fanners — fan dancers.

Mugg — staffer on *Variety*.

Cuffo-mugg — writer, such as myself, who contributes pieces to *Variety* anniversary issues.

Nsg — not so good (sometimes *nsh,* not so hot).

Tinter — movie in color.

Meller — melodrama.

B.o. — box-office which in turn, usually means profitable.

Pix — motion pictures.

Pratfall — a comedy device involving a fall on the prat. In former times this was spelled "prattfall," but Theodore Pratt, the novelist, conducted an all-out nationwide campaign

54

against the spelling and convinced everyone in the writing trade that *pratt,* as meaning the pratt, is spelled *prat.*

Fanny Rose Shore — true name of the ever delightful Dinah.

W.k. — well known.

Terp — *Varietyese* for terpsichorean.

Peeling — stripping, as in disrobing in front of an audience, shaking, at the same time, provocative portions of flesh; seldom practiced by men.

Yock dept. — area of mirth.

The Man Who C T D — a famous play about a man who c t d.

Brodies — takes a dive, falls, fails, peters out.

Cliff Nazarro — a movie actor skilled in double talk.

Celibate — unfortunate.

Paulmossed — cleaned up, censored; from Paul Moss, a former New York City official who struggled against smut in the theater, with the consequence that plays today are, in Tallulah's phrase, clean as the driven slush.

Nabe house — neighborhood movie theater.

Throw-in — second feature at a nabe house.

Unsapolio — to dirty up as against to paulmoss.

Humpty Dumpty — character who said, "When I use a word, it means just what I choose it to mean." Otherwise, Abel Green.

10. SIME'S HIDDEN-NOTE TRICK

QUITE A FEW years have gone by since I first heard of Sime's secret note-taking. The thing made a deep impression on me, probably because I spent nearly twenty years as a note-taking animal for various newspapers.

Sime was a man who never needed to use his last name, which was Silverman. He was the founder of *Variety,* and when they came to write his biography, they titled it *Lord Broadway.* He knew more about show biz than anybody alive in his era. He did a lot of the leg-work himself and one of the things he knew was that many people have a tendency to clam up when they see an interviewer taking notes. The person being interviewed suddenly becomes conscious of the fact that he is shooting off his face for publication and he gets either cagey or shy.

Sime solved the problem. He had some small scratch-pads made up and then supplied himself with plenty of stub pencils. He'd walk around Broadway and at, say, Forty-fifth Street, he'd come upon a couple of show-biz personalities engaged in conversation. He'd join them.

As bits of news evolved from the conversation, Sime just stood there, his hand in his coat pocket, and I imagine that some of the people figured he was a helluva lousy reporter not to be taking the stuff down. But he *was* taking it down. He had developed the knack of scribbling little notes *inside his coat pocket.*

The technique involved was somewhat similar to that employed by a famous surgeon I once read about. A visitor in his office noted that the surgeon kept his right hand inside a wooden box which sat on his desk. The box had a hole in it just large enough to admit his hand, and the surgeon continued fumbling with something inside all during his conversation with the visitor. Finally he was asked about the box, and he removed the lid. Inside were some cords, and the surgeon explained that he had been tying various knots in these cords, using only one hand and without being able to see what he was doing. It was necessary, he said, for him to reach inside a lot of folks and tie assorted knots and, more often than not, it wouldn't be a salutary practice for him to use both hands in the process.

56

Sime's note-taking was not, of course, as difficult a digital maneuver as the surgeon's knot-tying. But it was difficult enough. I always wanted to try it because I like to keep a record of conversations I sometimes have with people who do not know that I am a writer. One summer I got around to giving it a try. I acquired some stub pencils and some little scratch-pads. I went over to the Waldorf-Astoria and loafed around the lobby with my hat on — a defiant bit of nonconformism. After a while along came Edgar Bergen, an old friend from Beverly Hills, and I collared him. I shook hands and then ducked my right into my pocket, got hold of the pencil stub, and tried to get a sparkling and newsy conversation going. The first part of the Bergen interview consisted of erasures. Erasures of nothing. I had the stub pencil upside down and was erasing to beat hell on blank paper. Then Ted Saucier, who helped me build the Waldorf-Astoria back in the early 1930's, came on the scene and Edgar turned to speak to him and I got the pencil switched around.

Here is what I put down:

I want you to understand, if you don't understand it already, that Edgar Bergen is not a dull man and never has been a dull man. Those Sime-style notes represent an erudite and witty conversation but I'll just be damned if I know what it was about. I suspect that we talked about the gentle tolerance and the milk-mild compassion of W. C. Fields, as well as the extravagant spending of Rudy Vallee and the temperate habits of Bergen's neighbor, John Barrymore. I'm quite certain I asked him some questions, and that he answered them in his customary forthright manner. But it appears to me that the little pad must have been sort of whirling around in my pocket, so that my notes crisscross and overlap and collide head on. Well, I thought, a guy's got to learn. It's just like golf, or swimming, or sex, or making spaghetti sauce. You've got to keep at it a while before you get real good at it.

Bergen said it was time for him to take Charlie to the bathroom so we went on up to his suite and I waited around, smoked a cigarette, kept my hat on, and pretty soon along came Sherman Billingsley. Just the guy I was looking for. I was working on a magazine piece about tipping and Sherman agreed to give me a lot of authentic information. He stood and talked (hat in hand) and I scribbled furiously inside my pocket. Then he departed — I think he was on his way to the Waldorf kitchens to borrow a paring knife and a side of bacon. I pulled out my pad. It was blank. I stared at it a while, mystified and bewildered. Then I reached in my pocket again. I had scribbled the Billingsley remarks on a package of cigarettes and couldn't make a bit of sense out of them.

I cussed a little and made a mental note to go see Billingsley at his groggery. Then I checked the clock and took an elevator to keep an appointment with a great man, Mr. Harry Lillis Crosby.

This time I did my secret note-taking while sitting down and Bing was in good form. He spoke a lot of interesting and unorthodox opinions that I felt were worth preserving for posterity. Here are the notes I took:

I'm not sure, either. Not at all. My memory seems to tell me that Bing had something to say about Barney Dean, but it looks as if that part ran off the pad. It looks as if almost everything ran off the pad. There's something in all that mess about Jack Kapp, but for the life of me I can't make it out, nor can I remember it.

What I need is practice and I don't have the time, so I'm giving the whole project up. I might go ahead and perfect my technique except for one thing. When I had finished with Bing he walked to the elevator with me and just before the car arrived he gave me a funny look and said:

"It's none of my business, pal, but what you got in your coat pocket there — a mouse?"

That settled it.

11. DUMBO EXPLODES THE EXHAUST BOX

THE AMERICAN PEOPLE have always enjoyed the manner in which many foreigners produce multiple confusions whenever they undertake to write our language. It is my impression that the Japanese are leaders in the work of creating unintentional humor in this field. A friend once gave me a document which was being handed out to tourists in a Japanese city and which I reprinted in a book called *Waikiki Beachnik*. I have given myself legal authorization to print it again, as follows:

RULES OF THE ROAD IN JAPAN

At the rise of the hand of policeman, stop rapidly. Do not pass him or otherwise disrespect him.

When a passenger of the foot hove in sight, tootle the horn trumpet to him melodiously at first. If he still obstacles your passage, tootle him with vigour and express by word of mouth the warning, "Hi hi!"

Beware of the wandering horse that he shall not take fright as you pass him. Do not explode the exhaust box at him. Go soothingly by, or stop by the roadside till he pass away.

Give big space to the festive dog that make sport in the roadway. Avoid entanglement of dog with your wheel-spokes.

Go soothingly on the grease-mud, as there lurk the skid demon. Press the brake of the foot as you roll around the corners to save the collapse and tie-up.

I have now come into possession of another manuscript written by a Japanese art student in Los Angeles. This young man was taking a course in animated cartooning, in which the Disney Studio was cooperating extensively. The students were shown the feature film *Dumbo* and then required to write the answers to a series of questions concerning the story theme, the conflict, the major crisis, the climax, the plot, and so on.

Here is the paper turned in by the Japanese student:

Story theme is a short subject of melody constituting the bases of variation on small part to make use of. Also a composition or movement.

Conflict is a sharp disagreement, as of interesting or idea — conflict prepare — origin of action, cause and effect, static, jumping, rising movement, point of attack, transition, crisis, climax and resolution. I think color in Dumbo picture is conflict to another.

Climax is a series of ideas character, or events progressively increasing force and interesting or bring into climax.

Dumbo story.

As far I'm concerned, about the movies called Dumbo, the flying elephant. His life begin and took place at the circus which Dumbo was born late while Mrs. Jumbo name him as Dumbo. Of course Dumbo has a big ear and neighbor were disappointed, whisper because they never did see such small baby elephant has a large ear before.

On the circus parade, Dumbo was shy and of course he didn't know their will be crowd and cheer for him. So he look at the crowd than fall into the puddle of mud. Later, Mrs. Jumbo took Dumbo for bath of been so dirty. Then finish his bath so he'd play game with his mother. When the crowd came to visit the circus — one of the kids try to make trouble over Dumbo but sudden Mrs. Jumbo became angry and try to protect her son away from those trouble maker.

After Dumbo's mother lock up in mad house cage, Dumbo lost his mother and not able to see her again. Dumbo found himself alone, then Timothy the mouse meet Dumbo and heard about his mother's frantic. Timothy will be able to help Dumbo to get into the climax.

Next day, Dumbo got his first appearance debut — show. But there were accident while Dumbo slip into elephants stampede, was responsible for the show of damage and injurie person. In his second act, on stages with the funny clown portrayed the firemen to save Dumbo as a baby from the fire, was plugged into the mud bucket. Dumbo became embarrasing himself. After the show, every body celebrating and talk about Dumbo that he made a tremendous performance. But sadness poor Dumbo was hopeless. Timothy bought news for him that he'll be able to bring Dumbo to his mother. Although, Dumbo see her again was glad to her from long time — the love of her son to be proud of — happiness forever with forgiveness. Then they left to say goodbye to Dumbo's mother.

Same night, Dumbo and Timothy was drunk while they both drink alcohol water from the bucket of water which the bottle of wine fall into the bucket. Both of them having fun blowing bubble. Suddenly, they seen something strange on the bubble has change to design. Elephants form into the air. Individual marching and musical preview of most colorful elephant has created and develop by hundred.

In the morning, the crow land on the tree and whisper over Dumbo and timothy was up on the high tree. (but how could Dumbo got up there). So timothy wake up — and look at the crow — said "What are you doing down here." Tim look down and wake Dumbo up and fall from tree into the pond. The crow start to laugh and make fun of Dumbo and timothy but timmy was mad that they shouldn't laugh at Dumbo cause of loneliest and sadness as he told them. So they left the crow but the crow will able to help Dumbo to train to fly in the air with his big ear. The birds give Dumbo an magic feather. When Dumbo jump off from the cliff — he was flying.

Dumbo appear his performance as same act "The Fire house" with the clown. He drive the clown away by himself as he flying without magic feather. Then give him the idea to pay the clown back as he was.

And that all the story of Dumbo end became hero as timothy his manager.

I suggested from Mrs. Jumbo was angry (as mad elephant) and the part Dumbo was flying and chase the clown. I think the character are very concern about conflict, equivalent to action, personality and expression to the relationship.

On the staged to perfection, the scene — Bubble develop as an designing elephants — marching and musical are tremendous idea and good performance. Colorful design elephant form creation have movement.

Well, perhaps, Dumbo suppose to be on top of 5 or 6 elephant but accidental slip into the one of the elephant and here come the

stampede, fall, damage and injurie — is better staged action as far
I'm concerned.

12. *POO SEEP AND*
CHICKASEE FRICKEN

A MALAPROPISM, as we have noted before, is the misuse of a
word to produce a grotesque rhetorical effect. Mrs. Kenneth
Jones of Worden, Illinois, tells us of a friend who once spoke of
a young man "in a porcupine hat," when she meant that he was
wearing a pork-pie hat. This same lady, on another occasion,
announced that she had just bought an expensive black dress
"all covered with Seagrams." That is a lovely malapropism.

A spoonerism, however, is an altogether different thing. The
technical name for the making of a spoonerism is *metathesis,*
and it involves the accidental transposition of letters and sometimes of whole words. I once overheard a lady in a butcher shop
ask for "half a dozen chork pops." That was a spoonerism. It
derives its name from the Reverend William A. Spooner, for
many years warden of New College, Oxford. He died in 1930
at the venerable age of eighty-six and probably hent to weaven.
He was by reputation so prone to transpose sounds and letters
that he became famous locally, then his reputation spread
throughout England, and eventually his name passed into the
language, and you will find it today in the dictionaries and en-
cyclopedias.

Among the spoonerisms attributed to Mr. Spooner himself
were these:

"Let us now sing the hymn, Kinkering Kongs Their Titles
Take."

"The Lord is a shoving leopard."

"Mardon me, padam, but I think you are occupewing my pie."

"I remember your name perfectly but I just can't think of your face."

"It was indeed a blushing crow."*

Apparently a spoonerism is most likely to pop up among people who are engaged in formalized speech — people who are concentrating hard on what they are saying. Dr. Spooner made his in sermons. We hear them frequently from actors. And we encounter them all the time in the speech of radio and television announcers. Joe Ranson, an author and publicist, has for years made a hobby of collecting fine examples of fluffs and blunders among radio and TV performers. He has shown us, for example, that a single phrase can be spoonerized in two or more different ways. He remembers the announcer who said, "Why not try Betty Crocker's poo seep?" And he remembers the actress in a soap opera who, on shipboard, described the fog as being "as thick as sea poop." Poo seep, sea poop, soo peep — all three of them are splendid.

As an example of the transposition of whole words, Mr. Ranson tells of the sports announcer in Madison Square Garden who was describing the crowd. "Several," he said, "are quite dressed up. There are a number, in fact, in gownless evening straps."

The Ranson collection includes Milton Cross describing "The

* Bergen Evans tells me that during a research project in England he happened upon the truth about Dr. Spooner. The clergyman committed but a single spoonerism himself, according to the information Dr. Evans dug up. In a sermon Dr. Spooner intended to say something about a half-formed wish and it came out "half-warmed fish." Says Dr. Evans: "It was enough, of course, to add a word to the dictionary and enlarge the gaiety of nations and deservedly constitutes one of the most memorable moments of the pulpit. But it was the only spoonerism of which he himself was ever guilty." Bergen Evans, I might add, is a gentleman, a scholar, and a truthful and reliable man, and sometimes he is wrong about things.

64

Prince of Pilsen" as "The Pill of Princeton," and Mel Allen saying, "It's smipe poking time, gentlemen." And Jerry Lawrence once tossed this one off: "You will know the King and Queen have arrived when you hear a twenty-one-sun galoot."

A masterpiece among spooneristic utterances came from the lips of an emcee who started off by introducing Walter Pidgeon in this way: "Mr. Privilege, this is indeed a Pidgeon." The man was so flustered by his blunder that he went immediately into more turbulent waters, saying, "Our sponsor is the world's biggest manufacturer of magnoosium, aleeminum and stool."

Another announcer once spoke of "the Duck and Doochess of Windsor" and I myself heard a radio man, describing a parade, mention the approach of "the Girls' Bum and Droogle Corps." Not long ago a voice came out of my television set saying that the next program would be "in color and whack and blite."

Bennett Cerf knows an announcer who once introduced a musician as having been a veteran of the war in the "New Juinea gungles," and then said that the same young man, a flutist, was going to play a "slote flulo." And there's the famous case of the Los Angeles announcer who urged his audience to "always get the best in bread," but got it twisted.

An announcer named Fred Hoey opened his broadcast one day with this: "Good afternoon, Fred Hoey, this is everybody speaking." My friend J. Bryan, III, once collected a fine bunch of radio fluffs for the *Saturday Evening Post,* including Fred Hoey saluting himself, and certain announcers who said such things as "WOR presents the newted nose analyst . . ." and "The urge is needent." J. Bryan, III, who writes under the name of J. Bryan, III, although his real name is Joe Bryan, gave several instances in which the announcer, having committed one spoonerism, became so rattled that he followed it with a second. Lowell Thomas, for example, was doing a newscast one evening when he spoke of Ambassador Bull Billett." Mr. Thomas leaped quickly to the next item in his script, saying, "In England today, Sir Stifford Crapps . . ." During World War II one announcer spoke of "the battle of the Bulgian Belch" and an English radio man, describing a lesser engagement, said that "shores of skells were fired."

There have been, of course, many malapropisms to go with the spoonerisms committed in radio and TV. During Khrushchev's visit to our shores in 1960, I heard a television announcer, speaking in the customary gentled-down tone employed by those broadcasting from the United Nations chambers, speak as follows: "I'm sure you firks would . . . I'm sure you folks would like to know that . . ."

I've heard about another television man, whamming across a commercial, who addressed the housewives of the nation: "Does your husband wake up mornings dill and lustless?"

I am indebted to the public relations director of Alfred A. Knopf for one more. He told it to his assistant, who had lunch with Mary Metcalf and told Mary, and Mary told Ed Metcalf, and Ed told me, so it must be authentic. A cooking expert on radio was giving the ladies her recipe for vichysoisse. "Now," she said, "first you take a leek . . ."

A talent for both spoonerisms and malapropisms is by no means confined to the professionals. Almost everybody seems to have a relative or a friend possessing a genius for garbling words and sentences. A doctor telephoned me and told me that he knows a girl in upstate New York who speaks of a thing as being "real diculous," who says she thinks she would enjoy living in "New Braska," and who wants "to go to New York and see the Entire State Building."

Carol Hollingsworth of Seattle reports that her mother is expert at malapropisms. She was telling about a holdup committed by two soldiers. "And on top of all that," she said, "they were A. F. of L. from the army." There was a store nearby called

"The Three G. I. Joes," which she invariably referred to as "The Three-Eyed Joes."

Mrs. Vera M. Johnson of Fresno writes about a "wonderful old lady who described everything that was worn out, torn down or useless as *decrapitated*." This same old lady kept her house spotless because she was "algeric to dust."

Mrs. Robert E. Crebo of Dearborn, Michigan, tells us of a neighbor who always spoke of things as being "funny as a clutch" and who once described another woman: "There she stood with her arms and legs akimbo." To so stand would mean with the hands on the hips and also the feet on the hips. Try it.

Martha Simons of Philadelphia has a friend who says that so-and-so "looks like the raft of God," and another friend who once got her tongue so twisted that she said, "It's six a dozen and half a one of the other."

Mrs. William G. Patterson of Tacoma knows a woman who sometimes exclaims, "Woe and behold!" And Mrs. Alice M. Majeski of Topeka reports that a certain Kansas woman, referring to a sick friend, remarked, "The doctor says she's got nervous prostitution."

A lady in Wisconsin sent us a whole batch of blunders made by her mother. She spoke of an injured dog as "bleeding like a stuffed pig," and she sometimes told about how one of her sons served on "Anniweecock" during the war. At a wedding she said, "It's so good to have the whole family conjugated together again." She once spoke of visiting some people on "Lake Champagne" in New York State, and of meeting some people who came from "Armadillo, Texas."

Helen Wolfe of St. Louis once had a cleaning woman who spoke of a room as being "all tipsy-turvy," but when she got through with it, it was "spit and span." This same woman, describing all the troubles she'd had, summed it up with: "I've had to rape and scrape all my life to make ends meet."

Mrs. Doris D. Horn of Tullahoma, Tennessee, also reports

on a cleaning woman who was telling how she had tried to light a gas heater. "It exploded," she said, "and burned my eye-bowers off."

Mrs. M. Greenawalt of Baltimore writes us about a friend whose husband had some trouble with his knee, and who described it as being "something in his joists or tendrils." This same woman once asked Mrs. Greenawalt for advice on where to plant a Formosa tree.

Mrs. Mary Stagg Harrod of Frankfort, Kentucky, has a neighbor with a fine talent for malapropisms. She says that her little boy just loves to visit excavations "and watch them work with the bullnoser." She says that she's going to have "loogers" put in her attic for ventilation, and once at a bridge party she exclaimed, "Oh, look! There's one of those soup latrines that I've been trying to find."

Mrs. Ann K. Ligon of Dyersburg, Tennessee, knows several expert word-manglers. There's a cook who enjoys making "chicken in a camisole." Mrs. Ligon overheard a man in a supermarket asking for a bottle of "harmonized milk." She has a friend whose child got the colic and was given "a dose of paragarlic." And she knows a woman who spoke of a certain cocktail lounge as "a good place to drop by for a pick-up."

Most of the foregoing items are malapropisms, but my mail has also brought in scores of additional spoonerisms.* Carol Hollingsworth, for example, tells us that her sister once announced that she was going to get her soles half-shoed, and on another occasion asked if she might have a coff of cuppee.

Mrs. Pat Burrs of Dixon, Illinois, writes that about twenty

* In case you are wondering how I acquired all these items from people scattered over the country, I must explain that most of the malapropisms and spoonerisms in this book appeared originally in articles I did for *Good Housekeeping,* and after each article appeared, the readers showered me with more examples of blunders and fluffs. I have now run out the string on this subject and have no use for any more of them.

years ago she and her husband spent an evening at the Moody Bible Institute in Chicago. The next day her husband told someone, "We went last night to the Mighty Booble Institute." Mrs. Burrs said he's never been able to live it down, and that another of his spoonerisms came one evening when he turned on the radio "to hear Madame Human Shank."

Mrs. Alice L. Schwab of Paterson, New Jersey, reports that her sister is constantly producing spoonerisms. She says that "the jump's jointing" and speaks of the movie actor Rickey Mooney, and says "the whole koot and kabiddle." Watching a television drama one evening she remarked, "The thick plottens." (That could also be expressed, "The thot plickens.") This same sister once said, "I'd give anything right now for a plate of chickasee fricken." Mrs. Schwab, in passing, tells of a co-worker who, after a rest period, said, "Well, I guess I'll get back to the old grime."

Mrs. Doris Walsh of Webster, New York, tells us that a young friend of her son dashed into her house and announced that he had just won a prize, "a pound of Farmer's Fannie."

Mrs. Grace Stanforth of Tucson has a sister who, describing all the misfortunes of a friend, added, "and on top of all that she has vicious pernemia."

Mrs. T. H. Kirk of Oreland, Pennsylvania, tells one on herself — how she once described her dog as lying before the fire "with his turl cailed up."

My own friends and neighbors have been showering me with various examples of spoonerisms they themselves have committed or that were uttered by someone they know. A prize item is the one spoken by a woman who, telling a story to her children, described an Indian "who died and went to the happy grunting hound." Another neighbor told me that one evening in a literary discussion he mentioned John Steinbeck's book *The Rapes of Grath,* and on another occasion described a local citizen as being "a chillar of the purch." A woman I know told me that a' 'salesman rang her doorbell one day and her husband answered. The salesman said, "I'd like to speak to the hady of the louse." And this same woman's daughter, reciting the Declaration of Independence in school, spoke ringingly of "the hursuit of pappiness."

I remember a young deputy district attorney in Denver who once threw himself into confusion by saying, "Gentlemen of the jury, we intend to prove conclusively that this was a case of pre-murditated medder."

A man on the radio said, "Here comes Dick — look at that grin, splitting his ear from face to face." And a tennis official on television introduced Richard Nixon in this fashion, "Ladies and gentlemen, the Price Vesident."

I think, however, that my favorite spoonerism of them all was sent in by Mrs. Frances M. Gilligan of Washington, D.C. Mrs. Gilligan reports on a friend who walked into a drugstore and asked for "a jar of odorarm deunderant."

That's what I call a snooperism!

13. COLONEL SPEAKNAGLE STOOPLING

COLONEL Lemuel Q. Stoopnagle, a man unhappily gone from the national scene, usually introduced himself on radio by spoonerizing his name. Sometimes it might be twisted about as above; again it came out "Naglestoop Speakling," or "Speak-stagle Poopling."

His true name was Frederick Chase Taylor and he was as good a writer of humor as he was a performer onstage or on the air. He started out as a Wall Street broker. The house fell down on him in 1929 and there was not much broking for him to do after that so he took a job in Buffalo as a radio continuity writer.

Taylor was sitting at his typewriter one morning when the Muse of Comedy, a lady named Thalia, walked in and busted him one with a bladder. Something had gone wrong with the CBS line hooking the station to the network and a fifteen-minute period had to be filled. An announcer named Budd Hulick burst in on Taylor and explained the nature of the emergency. In a few minutes the two men were on the air and one of the most popular comedy acts in radio's history was born.

For eight years, in the 1930's, Stoopnagle & Budd entertained the American public. Then the team split up and the two men went their separate ways in radio. Stoopnagle was a thickset man with a cherubic face, a rarity among comedians of the time in that he was a college graduate, and he was frequently as funny off-mike as he was on the air. He could play but one song on the harmonium, "I Love Coffee, I Love Tea," and that became his theme. He had an extraordinarily inventive mind and while he loved the reverse English involved in spoonerisms, his clever way of dealing with the language sometimes approached sheer genius.

Usually on the radio show his partner Budd would ask him if he had any new inventions to describe, and he always did. Among them were these:

A twenty-foot pole, for not touching a guy you wouldn't touch with a ten-foot pole . . . twice.

A wrist watch with a whistle on it, in case someone came up and asked, "Hey, you got a wrist watch with a whistle on it?"

An upholstered deep, for sailors to fall asleep in them.

Eyeglasses with vertical stripes on them, so bank tellers can recognize their customers when they meet them outside the cage.

A daisy with only the she-loves-me petals on it, so she always loves you.

A square bathtub for not getting rings in it.

71

Then there were the Colonel's definitions — masterpieces in the art of lexicography. Here are some samples:

A straw is stuff that you drink a soda through two of them.

A clock is something they have in an office so you can tell how late you wish you weren't in the morning, what time you go to lunch before and come back after, and how long before you can start stopping work and begin to end the day's work by stalling along until.

The Pacific Ocean is what the United States is between the Atlantic and.

Afternoon is what if you were out late last night, you'd better hurry or you won't be up until.

A fortnight is a thing that, in an English play, somebody hasn't seen Lord Plushbottom in a, practically.

Gasoline is stuff that if you don't use good in your car it won't run as well as if.

Ambidextrose: being able to buy either granulated or lump sugar.

Storkings: hose for girls with long, thin legs.

Possecat: a cat who hunts mice with a gun.

Downholsterer: a man who tears sofas apart.

Flatlas: a map of the world before Columbus.

Pregnosticator: a doctor who tells you if you are going to have a baby.

Prograsstinator: man who keeps putting off mowing his lawn.

Banguet: dinner for a bunch of firecracker manufacturers.

Chowmaine: potatoes.

Knocktet: eight woodpeckers.

Halfbreathe: an Indian with one nostril.

Hoosiery: stockings made in Indiana.

Champagnezee: man who makes a monkey of himself in night clubs.

Manokleptiac: a guy who backs into a department store, puts stuff on the counter and runs like anything.

Porcuprone: a porcupine lying face down.

Colonel Stoopnagle once advanced the brash opinion that parades, as conducted on the streets of our towns and cities, are not properly organized. Each person on the sidelines may have a particular section of a parade he wants to look at longer than the other sections — perhaps he has a friend or a relative in that section, or he may be the man who designed the costumes, or made the flags, or decorated the floats. The section he particularly wants to see goes past him before he has a chance to take it all in and if he wants to study it further, he has to sort of trot alongside it, and stand the risk of being brought up for disorderly conduct. The Colonel proposed that all future parades be formed up along a stretch of Fifth Avenue, or whatever street they ordinarily use, and that the marchers and floats and bands and horsemen and cops and everybody else in the parade stand still, so the onlookers could walk around them and take their time looking at the sections they liked best.

Stoopnagle once described Lowell Thomas as "a man whom posterity will recognize as the Lowell Thomas of his time." He wrote about Old Doctor Ther, famous for having invented the Ther Mometer. He said New Jersey was what Governor Moore was Governor Moore of.

Here are a few of his immortal utterances:

Look at the haircut I need.
That man over there is the woman whose penthouse we went up to the other night's husband.
If it weren't for half the people in the United States, the other half would be all of them.
For a man who reads as much as I do, I read very little.
He's a brother-in-law of the man who lost his job's wife.
The United States, as I like to call this great country of ours . . .
She's visiting the man who went to the ball game's mother.

The Colonel was author of a series of classical stories in which the spoonerism was given a heavy workout. Some of these were grouped under the heading "Tairy Fales for the Fittle Lokes — and Bigger Toople, Peep." Some of these stories were "Wink Van Ripple," "The Pee Little Thriggs," "Paul Revide's Rear," and "Little Ride Hooding Red."

Some of the foregoing Stoopisms are taken from a book the

73

Colonel published in 1944, titled *You Wouldn't Know Me from Adam*. In that book he told of a man named Jinguel Q. Stoopjangle who came to him seeking a job as a songwriter.

Outlining his qualifications, Mr. Stoopjangle said that he had written the lyrics to *do, re, mi, fa, sol, la, ti, do*. Originally, he said, he had written it, *da, da, da, da, da, da, da, da*.

"People used *da, da, da,* and so on for a while," said Mr. Stoopjangle, "but the hurt look in their eyes prompted me to try to make the words more interesting."

"Do you think *do, re, mi,* et cetera, is more interesting?" asked the Colonel.

"When you compare them with my earlier effort, yes," said the lyricist. "Try singing *ga, gee, gram, dun, wham, sag, lee, ga* and you'll understand why all singers use my *do, re, mi,* et cetera."

The Colonel died in 1950 at the age of fifty-two and I, for one, miss him a lot.

14. *SMALL*

A writer of our time needs a lot of courage to set down a story about an animal that talks, particularly any story involving a talking dog. I am a nonconformist with knobs on. Some years ago I produced a short story about a talking dog, and my scribbling friends all laughed at me until the editors of a national magazine bought it and published it. I got a ton of mail from people who read it and since it is concerned with a special aspect of language, I think it has a place in this book. I offer then, the story of Small.

WE ALWAYS say that Small has a bigger vocabulary than any other dog we know about. When I say "shortstop" to him he knows what I mean. He heads immediately for the stone wall out by the garage. The driveway runs up to this wall and we take our positions on the pavement. I stand about thirty feet back and Small takes his place facing the wall, perhaps six feet away from it, the black stub of his tail erect and trembling. He'll stand there forever without moving a step, so long as he knows I'm behind him. I shoot the hard rubber ball along the pavement, sometimes throwing it hard and sometimes using a change-up. The face of the wall is rough so the direction of the rebound is unpredictable; but as that ball comes off the surface, Small is on it like a cat. He takes it straight in his teeth if it's a line drive; he catches it over his shoulder, going away; but his greatest skill is in handling a Baltimore chop. He has perfected a knack of catching it when it comes off the pavement in a high bounce, letting it clunk against the roof of his mouth. Everybody who sees him says he's better than Rizzuto, and I've often remarked that if I could teach him to throw to first, I'd have the greatest shortstop on earth — a dog to compare with Honus Wagner.

We've never kept count of the words he knows. The Wheelers, up the road, have a Scottie named Angus and they claim he has a bigger vocabulary than Small. They write down all the words he understands in a little book which they call "Angus's Dictionary," and whenever company comes they get it out and start reading all the words in it. We like the Wheelers except for this one bad trait — their eternal bragging on their dog. They say Angus knows the word "caterpillar" but I don't believe it. If you want a dog to know about a caterpillar, you make it simple and call it a worm. There's no necessity for a dog to know all the varieties of worms, unless worms are the only wildlife you have around your place. Small knows "worm" and "deer" and "squirrel" and "frog" and "turtle" and even "fox." If I say to him, "Go get that turtle!" he scampers off across the fields, searching the grass for a turtle. The same with deer, and frog, and squirrel, and fox. The Wheelers had the gall to tell me one day that Small doesn't actually distinguish between these words — that when I say, "Go get that turtle!" he heads into the fields expecting to find anything from a chipmunk to a camel. They said the tone of my voice, not the actual words, is the thing that sends him on his way. This from people who say their dog knows that the word "caterpillar" means a caterpillar!

Small is a black cocker, now nine years old, and has been with Betsy and me all but five weeks of his life. Before we got him we didn't care much for dogs, but now we carry on like a couple of fools. As much as I try to avoid it, I can't keep from talking a kind of baby talk to him.

Small almost never sets foot off our property but a week ago Tuesday he disappeared. I'll be truthful about it — I was as upset as if a child of mine had vanished, and so was Betsy. Her brother, Reed Poovey, was visiting us at the time and I couldn't keep from thinking that his presence had something to do with Small's disappearance. He's a chemist with a big pharmaceutical laboratory down in Pennsylvania and while I couldn't smell anything on him, I had an idea that Small could, and that Small didn't like it, and just made up his mind to take a walk for a while and get away from it.

We alerted the police all over the county, but I don't think they did anything more than write it down on a piece of paper. A man pays his taxes and supports these big lugs and when he needs them to find a dog, all they do is set around and play pinochle and maybe poke tickets under your windshield wiper when they ought to be out scouring the forests and fields, as I was. I spent two days threshing around in the woods and even got mired in the swamp over toward the parkway and came back with mud up to my hips. Not a trace of Small. Then on the third morning, just as daylight was breaking, I heard the whimpering at the back door and there he was — covered with burs and mud and brambles — the sorriest looking animal you ever saw.

He was ravenously hungry, which told us he hadn't eaten all the time he was gone. We fed him and soothed him with talk and after a while he quit trembling and flopped himself on the floor and went to sleep.

There was something enormously frustrating about not knowing where he had been. "I'd give anything in the world right now," I said, "if he could only talk."

"Wouldn't it be wonderful!" exclaimed Betsy. "We'll never know where he's been all that time, what he's been doing. If he could just sit down and tell us all about it!"

Reed Poovey was reading the morning paper. Now he looked up.

"You want him to talk?" he asked.

"That's what I said," I answered, rather abruptly. I was still a little cool toward him.

"Suppose I told you," said Reed, "that maybe we could fix it so he can talk?"

"Please, Reed," said Betsy.

"I just happened to remember," Reed went on, "about Doctor Vorpek. He's a queer sort of guy who's been doing some special work down at our lab. Comes from somewhere in the Middle East. Keeps pretty much to himself, but I've had several long talks with him. He told me once about a formula that'll make a dog talk. He spent a couple of years in Tibet and one day he ran into an old native who had a dog that talked. The old guy took a shine to Vorpek and told him he had a formula that would make most dogs capable of talking, and Vorpek got it from him. I don't actually vouch for it, but I think I could get the formula if you want to try it on Small."

We laughed at him at first, but after a while I got to thinking about the number of times I had expressed the wish that Small could talk, and I began asking questions. Would it hurt the dog? Reed didn't think so. Would the dog talk English? Reed said he understood the dog would talk the language of its master. What precisely did it do to the dog physiologically? Reed wasn't sure — he said he thought it stiffened and constricted the animal's tongue, and that there was an ingredient in it that did something to the speech center in the brain.

When I began to show more than passing interest, Reed got on the phone and talked to Dr. Vorpek in Pennsylvania. He had quite an argument with the Doctor. Here was this Vorpek with a formula which he said would make a dog talk, and he told Reed over the phone that he didn't think dogs *ought* to talk, that it wouldn't be a good thing for the civilized world if they *could* talk. But Reed stayed with him and in the end came away from the phone with a sheet of paper that had an assortment of unreadable scrawls on it.

"So what happens next?" I wanted to know.

"You just take it to your druggist," Reed said. "It's the same as a prescription. You get three capsules and you give Small one every hour till he's taken all three. Then, about twenty-four hours later, if Vorpek is right, he'll begin to talk."

I took the paper and looked at it. Couldn't make a thing out of the hieroglyphics, except that they somehow looked frightening. Reed wanted to go ahead with the thing immediately, but I had changed my mind. I was afraid of it. Reed got a little sore and the next morning climbed into his car and started for home.

We still had the paper, and every time I looked at it I seemed to grow more restless. At last I drove down to the village and handed it to Doc Klem, the druggist. Doc took it and studied it a few moments and then looked up at me and said, "I can't figure out whether you're tryin' to kill silverfish or cure concrete."

"Is it poison?" I asked him.

"No," he said. "I wouldn't say it's poison. What's it for?"

I couldn't very well tell him that it was a prescription for making a dog talk English.

"My brother-in-law's a chemist," I told him, "and that's a special formula he's worked out for . . . well, I've got athlete's foot and he says this'll clear it up."

Doc studied it again. "Maybe so," he said, "but I wouldn't use it on myself. Might shrivel your toes up."

"You don't put it on your toes," I said quickly. "It's to be taken internally."

"That's worse yet," said Doc. "It's my guess it'll make you sick as a dog."

"I'll try it anyway," I said, and he went back behind and rattled bottles and in about ten minutes handed me the three capsules.

I took them home and laid them on the mantel and we debated the thing all afternoon. Betsy at first was dead set against giving them to Small for fear they would kill him. Yet there was something eating at her and it finally came out. "Just think," she said, "of the money we could make if he could talk."

I hadn't once thought of the money possibilities. I just wanted my dog to talk to me. I didn't like this idea of looking at it from the commercial side and I was about to say so when she said maybe she ought to take one of the capsules herself, just to make certain.

"Your own brother," I argued, "told you they wouldn't hurt Small, and Doc Klem said they weren't poison. That means they won't kill you. But they might do something else to you. They might work in reverse. You take one and you might start barking like a dog and scratching yourself with your hind leg."

"Quit trying to be a card," she said.

By the next day we had made the decision. We gave him the three capsules, an hour apart, and then stood nervously by in case he got sick, but he didn't. They worked on him like sleeping pills and he was dopey all evening. The following morning he spurned the biscuit we offered him for breakfast and when I got home from work Betsy said he had been following her around and *glaring* at her. At six in the evening she gave him his dinner. He walked up to the bowl and looked at it and then turned and gave Betsy a long stare and walked away from it.

I was in the living room looking at a magazine when he came in and hopped onto the divan.

"Get . . . down . . . offa . . . there!" I ordered, using the stern tone reserved for this sort of violation of the rules.

"Says who!"

I almost fell out of my chair. The two words were as distinct as any human being ever uttered them. I yelled for Betsy and she came running in from the kitchen. Small sat and looked from one to the other of us and Betsy, in a shrill, excited voice, cried out, "Tan my ittle boy talk?"

"Please, Betsy," said Small, "will you lay off that baby talk? Certainly I can talk. You wanted me to talk, didn't you? And now that I *can* talk, I've got something to say to you. Listen to me, Hervey Gregg. I don't want to be nasty about it, but I intend to sit on this divan whenever I feel like it. Where do you get this stuff of exiling me to the floor? Why don't *you* get down and crawl around on the floor for a while? Live your life in a forest of chair legs, see how you like it."

We were so aghast at this long speech that we gave him no argument about the divan. We just sat and stared at each other, and then at him.

"Turn on the TV," he said.

"Why, Small," said Betsy, "you never paid any attention to TV before. Can you see it? Can you tell what's going on?"

"Certainly," said Small. "Do you think I'm a moron, and blind in the bargain? I never paid any attention because of the lousy programs you tune in. From now on, I think I ought to get a vote on what we look at. Now, just one minute." He hopped off the divan and walked over to the big chair that stands directly opposite the television set. "This'll be my TV chair," he said, "and I want another cushion put on it — it's not quite high enough — and move it in toward the set about two feet."

It was *my* TV chair, but I let it pass, and said, "Which programs do you want to see, Small?"

"Wrestling," he said. "I like the wrestling. And when there's no wrestling, I'll take baseball."

"Now listen," I said, "I look at baseball a lot and you've never shown any interest."

"Of course not," he said. "I like to look at *big-league* baseball. How you can sit and watch those Yankees is beyond me. From now on, I want the Dodger games."

A woman, I suppose, adjusts herself to a situation quicker than a man. At any rate, Betsy spoke up. "Small, you didn't touch your dinner. You go right out there and eat your dinner and then we'll tune in some wrestling for you."

"Go on!" I snapped, trying to reassert my authority.

"Go eat it yourself," he said. "Horse meat and kibbled food! Yee — urp! Night after night after night. Hasn't it ever occurred to you that I'd like a little variety in my meals? Betsy, you got any chopped steak in the freezer?"

"Why, yes, but . . ."

"Drag 'er out!" said Small. "I want it cooked in a sort of cake, like a hamburger steak, and then I want two chocolate bars crumbled up and sprinkled over it."

81

"Now, just a minute!" I said.

"Please don't give me any argument," said Small. "I'm not being unreasonable. I've got rights, and I'm standing on them. Go ahead, Betsy, and fix my dinner."

Betsy hesitated, but I nodded to her and she went into the kitchen. Small and I sat looking at each other.

"Small," I finally said, "we're tickled to death that you can talk now. We've always wanted you to talk. You know we love you, and this talking will bring us even closer together. But I think we ought to have an understanding right now. You can't take charge of things here. You can't run the house."

"I'm not trying to run the house, Hervey," he said. "I've been leading a dog's life for a long time, and I don't like it. If you and Betsy will just be reasonable, we'll have no trouble. There's this matter of the food. There's this matter of sitting on the divan. And there's the matter of sleeping in the basement. We've got a perfectly good guest room upstairs, haven't we? Well, that's where I want to sleep from now on. *On the bed!* No more of that crummy old blanket in that raggedy old clothes basket in that clammy old basement!"

I had to put my foot down. A man can't let anyone, not even a dog, become a tyrant in his home.

"Small," I said, "you're going to sleep in the basement, as always. And you're not going to order Betsy and me around. You might as well get that straight right now."

He threw back his head and laughed; a sardonic, devilish laugh — an astonishing performance! He laughed so hard that tears came in his eyes and he wiped them away with his shaggy forepaws.

"I'm sleeping in the guest room," he finally said. "You try to get me in that basement again, and I'll fix *your* wagon!"

Now I laughed, scornfully. "Look who's talking!" I said.

"You try to get me in that basement," Small repeated, "and I use the one weapon I've got. I go to the neighbors. Man, oh

82

man! What I can tell the neighbors about the things that go on in this house! Hervey and Betsy Gregg, the happiest couple in North Westchester! What a laugh! Listen, big boy, I've had my eyes open for a long time. *And* my ears! Why, you drunken bum, I'll . . ."

"Wait a minute," I interrupted him. I knew he had us. I knew he could ruin us with the neighbors, now that he could talk. Betsy and I don't fight any more than other couples, but he'd exaggerate, just as he exaggerated now, calling me a drunken bum.

"I don't see any reason," I finally said, "why you shouldn't have the guest room. Except, of course, when we have guests."

"We'll take that up when we get to it," said Small. "I might give you a hint, though. I don't like the type of people you have as friends."

So we installed him in the guest room and the first thing he ordered was that the table radio be put on the floor and in no time at all he was able to turn it on and tune from station to station, using both front paws. Every time he came to a station that was playing music, either popular or classical, he'd snort and growl and move on until he located a panel show. "I've got sensitive ears," he said, as if we didn't already know it, "and this stuff you people call music is enough to drive a dog mad. If you only realized how horrible it really sounds . . . and that goes for *all* of it."

He had that radio on for the next two hours and we couldn't get to sleep. Once I got up and went in and asked him to please keep it low. He told me to go where it's hot. "You got a nerve," he said, "the nights you and your friends have kept me awake, yelling and singing and beating those horrible noises on that piano!" After a while he couldn't get anything but music so he turned it off and the house quieted down.

"He's getting meaner by the hour," I whispered to Betsy.

"We've got to do something," she said.

"Yes," I agreed, but I didn't know what.

The next ten days were like a nightmare. We hadn't considered all the bad things that go with talking. He could talk, so he could laugh, but not a pleasant laugh — always a sarcastic, howling laugh. And he could cry. Not as dogs whimper, but real human-style weeping and blubbering. And complain! He groaned and whined about a sore throat, about a paw that hurt, about a sting he got from a yellow jacket, about the misery of his youth and middle age. He griped about things we did. He gave Betsy a bitter dressing down for saying he had left his calling card somewhere. "If you ever use that expression about me again," he said, "I'll leave and you'll never find me." He was constantly whining for attention. "Come on out and play shortstop!" he'd say. "I want a malted milk!" he'd wail. "Go on downtown and get me some frankfurters!" he'd demand.

It was even worse when he was in an amiable mood. In age he's reckoned elderly and, like elderly humans, he spent hours reminiscing, reliving his past. He'd trail us around, talking, talking, talking. The trouble was, all his reminiscences were so dull. He really had nothing worth while to remember. The time he bit the Wilson dog on the leg and sent him kiting for home (he didn't remember the various bouts he had *lost*); the time he caught the baby squirrel and what a lot of fun he had refusing to give it up to me; the time he found the bone a foot and a half long down in the Granville woods, and so on and so on and so on. Lord, but I got sick of it!

Several times I tried to bring him into line with threats. I threatened that I'd sell him to a vaudeville act, and he said nothing would suit him more — he was fed up with this secluded life. I threatened to chain him in the basement until he learned manners. "Just try it," he said, "and I'll scream and howl bloody murder all night long, every night."

Nobody knew we had a dog that could talk. Small always remained silent when anyone was around. There was one experience, however, that I looked forward to — letting the Wheelers hear him speak, letting them see what an inferior mutt their Angus really was. So we asked them to stop by one afternoon, and I told Small I wanted him to walk up to them and start talking about something — the weather, politics, anything at all.

The Wheelers arrived and, as was the custom, Angus ran into the yard and began romping around Small. Small wouldn't even look at him — just lay there on the grass.

"Something wrong with Small?" asked Wheeler.

"Not a thing," I said, grinning. "He's just studying out a speech he has to make before the Rotary Club." I winked at Betsy.

We went in the house, leaving the dogs outside, and I was mixing cocktails in the dining room when I happened to glance through the window. Angus was standing with his head cocked to one side, staring at Small, who was still lying on the grass. I saw Small's eyes — he was rolling them around in his head — and his jaws were moving. Angus cocked his head first to one side, then to the other, and I could tell that Small was beginning to talk faster and louder, and that he was abusing his visitor. Suddenly he leaped to his feet and now he began yelling as he moved catlike toward Angus, and the language he was using can't be repeated here. Angus stood transfixed for a moment, then let out a dog scream, and took off.

Wheeler leaped from his chair. "Somebody's after the dogs!" he yelled, and made for the door. "I heard 'em! Come on, Gregg!" He rushed into the yard, shouting for Angus. Small was back lying on the grass, pretending that nothing had happened. I hurried over to him.

"Where's Angus!" I demanded. "Come on, tell me!" He just lay there, wiggling his tail. Wheeler gave me a funny look and then began racing around the outside of the house, calling for Angus. Gert Wheeler was right at his heels and beginning to get hysterical. Wheeler was howling that he had heard men talking outside and that Angus had been kidnaped, and they jumped in their car and roared away.

I really lost my temper. I gave it to Small good. But pretty soon the phone rang and it was Gert Wheeler, saying they had found Angus at home, cowering in a corner of the garage, whimpering and shivering. She was sobbing, and said they thought someone had poisoned him, and Wheeler had rushed off with him to the vet's.

I went back to Small and demanded to know what he had said to Angus. "Oh," he said casually, "I just gave him a good piece of my mind. Never did like him. But he didn't understand a word I said. Talk about dumb!"

So we went through it again, with Betsy and me threatening him, and he threatening us, and again he won.

The pay-off came the next morning, Sunday. Betsy and I were having an early breakfast when Small walked in.

"I want to go to church," he said.

"Now, Small . . ." Betsy began.

"I said I want to go to church, and I'm going to church."

"There's no point in your going to church," I argued. "Don't you know that dogs don't have souls?"

"Who said so?" he demanded. "How do you know?"

"You just don't, that's all," said Betsy. "Now forget about going to church."

"I *feel* like I've got a soul," he insisted. "And anyway, even if we dogs don't have souls, we like to *pretend* that we've got them. It's a comfort to us."

The argument got heated, and he finally announced that this was the day he was going up and down the road and blab to the neighbors, so at last I got on the phone and talked to the Reverend Claypool.

"This is a rather unusual request," I said, "but would it be all right if we brought our dog to services this morning?"

86

"My dear Mr. Gregg," he said, "you should know better than that. Of course you can't. You should know that we can't have dogs running around in church. Why on earth do you want to bring him in the first place?"

"Well, he . . ." I almost said that Small had asked to come to church, but caught myself. "He's not too well," I finally said, "and I just have a feeling I'd like to bring him. I'll keep him on a leash."

"I'm sorry," said Mr. Claypool. "The answer is no. If you did it everybody would want to do it."

Small went into a tantrum when he heard the decision, and *we* didn't even get to church. He raged and stormed and then began ripping the upholstery off the furniture. I'd had enough. I went upstairs and got a quilt and came down and went after him. It took me a while, but in the end I got the quilt over him and wrapped around him. We took him down in the basement and had to fight him every inch of the way, even though he was inside that quilt, and finally we got the chain on him.

"You'll never sleep again as long as I live!" he screamed at us, and we knew what he meant. Panting and perspiring, we trudged back upstairs and sat down.

"Go get Reed Poovey on the phone," I said. Betsy put in the call and I talked to him. I begged him, almost sobbing, to get in touch with Dr. Vorpek and find out how we could stop Small from talking.

"How long has he been at it?" Reed wanted to know. We counted up. "Thirteen days," I said.

"Well," said Reed, "I don't understand you people sometimes, but I already know how to stop him. Just leave him alone. The talking period lasts exactly two weeks. At the end of two weeks he quits, and goes back to normal. You'll have to get the prescription filled again. You still got the paper?"

"Yes," I yelled into the phone. "I've still got the paper, but I'm going to burn it the moment I hang up!"

"What's he been talking about?" Reed wanted to know.

"Church!" I howled. "Good-by!"

Betsy bawled me out — it wasn't her brother's fault — I was the one who had said I wanted Small to talk. I was so happy about the news that I apologized and told her I'd apologize to Reed.

Then I went to the basement and stood there and taunted Small. I didn't tell him what was going to happen. Anyway, he wasn't listening to me — he was trying to shout me down with his threats.

"Go ahead and yell!" I told him. "Yell your fool head off! You're not worrying me!"

The rest of the day he was quiet — saving his energy for night, and when he heard us go upstairs to bed he started. He bayed, and howled, and screamed, and threshed about on the chain, and then along about three in the morning the noise from below began to diminish, and finally died away altogether.

When I went to the basement at eight, he was sleeping. I reached out and touched him with my toe. He woke up and raised his head and looked at me, and the old affection was in his eyes, and his tail was wagging. I went back to the kitchen and got a biscuit and took it to him and he ate it.

He seemed to be very tired for a couple of days and spent a lot of time sleeping. Then he returned to his old ways, returned to his basket in the basement, returned to horse meat and kibbled food, returned to life in the forest of chair legs, returned to dozing while I watched the Yankees. He was exactly the same as he was in the days before we gave him the capsules, and gradually Betsy and I got ourselves adjusted.

About a week later Betsy was in the kitchen and I heard her say, "Oh, darn!" I called out and asked what it was, and she came to the living room door.

"We never did remember to ask him where he went the time he disappeared for two days," she said.

"Baby," I said, "I don't wanna know!"

15. HOW I WON THE CHAMPIONSHIP

YOU REALLY want to know? Well, then, twist my arm. The left arm, please — I won the title with my right.

Not long ago I read in a trade magazine that John O'Hara was asking $750,000 for the movie rights to his most recent book and that, if he got it, this would cipher out to a payment of $11.50 a word. Actually Mr. O'Hara would be making much more than that per word, because the sale of the book itself was not included in the figure. He might even get as much as $25 per word. There was a strong implication in the magazine that Mr. O'Hara's pay-per-written-word was a thing without precedent.

Yeh?

The magazine item took me back to an earlier day when I read in a metropolitan journal that the Duke of Windsor had been paid, for his memoirs, a greater sum per word than any other writer had ever received in history.

Yeh?

I don't know how much money they gave the Duke for serializing his book; nor do I know how much he got in book royalties. If it came to anything less than a million dollars or so, he's still the runner-up. I'm the Champ.

Perhaps you can remember back to the days when Calvin

Coolidge chose to write a syndicated column, and the great publicity attending that decision. Much was made of the fact that the former President was to get one dollar a word for every word he wrote. That was pure publicity; nobody who writes a syndicated column is ever paid by the word — his income fluctuates according to the number of newspapers that use his column and the size of those newspapers. The fact is, Coolidge made considerably more than a dollar a word with his column. The idea got into the popular imagination, however, that he was being handed a buck for every word he put down, and people exclaimed over it and it was considered a big and wondrous thing.

Now, as for the Duke of Windsor and his rate-per-word. I hereby challenge him to try to match my own achievement. I'm willing to put my cards on the table, to reveal all the details of the transaction through which, I feel quite certain, I gained the world's championship. In doing so I must confess that the thing which I wrote and which gave me the title was of even greater unimportance than anything Calvin Coolidge ever wrote at a dollar or more a word. I might even go so far as to say that the thing I wrote was of lesser consequence than the memoirs of the Duke of Windsor.

One day in 1947 the late Fred Allen was a guest at my home in upper Westchester County. During the afternoon he engaged in a long and hilarious monologue concerning the tribulations of a top comedian in radio. Among other things he made mention of the fact that he was having a terrible time getting adequate guest stars to appear on his radio show.

Impulsively I spoke up. "I'll be a guest on your program," I said, "provided you let me write my own script."

He surprised me by showing immediate interest. "Do you have an idea for a script?" he wanted to know.

"Sure," I said.

"Swell! How long will it take you to write it?"

90

"I can write it right now."

"Oh, no," he protested. "Don't bother about it today. Take your time with it — take a week or two."

"No," I said, "I can write it right now, and I'm going to write it right now."

I got paper and pencil and wrote one line. It was:

I have nothing to say.

I handed it to him and he studied it with an expression of perplexity and then I explained how I thought it could be used. He would give me a big slam-bang introduction as an author, and say that I had been on my way to some distant land when my journey was interrupted by an appeal from him to appear on his radio show, and that I had hopped a plane in San Francisco and hurried back to New York in order that I *could* make this important appearance, and then he would introduce me. The studio announcer would signal the audience for a large burst of applause, after which I would step to the mike and say:

I have nothing to say.

Fred thought it would make a good stunt and would serve as a satirical comment on the hordes of guest stars, especially ham-bone book authors, who face the microphones and beat their gums together briskly even though they, too, have nothing to say. It was good, too, because it would take up less than a minute of valuable program time. He scheduled it for a specific Sunday night and copied my five-word line into the script for that program.

There was the usual script conference a few days before the broadcast, attended by an assortment of network people and representatives of the sponsor and the advertising agency. It is axiomatic in radio as well as in Hollywood that no piece of writing can ever go through to the end the way it was originally written. There are too many people involved, people with authority and very little to exercise it on. Somewhere along the line everything has to be changed. Everything. Thus they arrived, in the script conference, at my single line, and a dozen heads went to work on it, trying to puzzle out ways of changing it, and finally one of the masterminds got it. Instead of *I have nothing to say* he decided it should be *I have nothing whatever to say*. The change was penciled in and incorporated in the revised script. I knew nothing about it until I arrived at the studio just before the program; and even then I thought nothing of it — the addition of the word *whatever* brought neither anguish nor joy to my breast. I scarcely noticed it.

So it went on the air and was a great success to half the radio audience, and a great enigma to the other half. I got many letters from people wanting to know what we meant — saying they thought it was awfully stupid to fly all the way back from San Francisco and get on a nationwide network and then say nothing; and a few who had a theory that I was drunk and *couldn't* say any more. Such letters I noisily consigned to the septic tank. On the other hand, those who got the point were enthusiastic and these included, strangely enough, several members of that bored fraternity, the radio columnists.

About a week after the broadcast I was startled when a letter came informing me that I was being paid five hundred dollars for that one line. I protested. I said I had expected nothing and wanted nothing and would take nothing — that the publicity for my books was easily a sufficient wage. But the protests were ignored and the money was sent to me and I kept it.

Then, quite suddenly, it occurred to me that this thing was a major literary achievement. I dug up an old arithmetic which my children had used in elementary school and studied for a couple of hours, and after that went to work with pencil and paper, and in the end figured out that I had been paid eighty-three dollars and thirty-three cents per word.

Now, suppose the Duke of Windsor had accepted my challenge and hauled out his ledger and let us look at it, and it turned out that he got *more* than $83.33 a word for his memoirs. I feel certain he didn't, but let's suppose he did. Morally and ethically I believe I still had him. When I was doing that arithmetic problem I got pretty sore about the interpolation of that word *whatever* into my line. Not for any aesthetic reason — it was simply a matter of economics. If those bums hadn't tampered with my script, my rate per word would have been an even one hundred dollars. As it was, they had reduced my rate by sixteen dollars and sixty-seven cents per word. There was no good reason for it. They just *had* to change something. For all I know the addition of that *whatever* may have destroyed the rhythmic flow and beauty of my prose. But that, at the moment, is not very important.

After I had thought about the thing for a while, I realized that the script conference had not actually injured me. The fact stands that when I wrote that line *it had only five words in it*. Five simple little words. Somebody else added that other word, *whatever*. Somebody else wrote it . . . I didn't; so that actually, from the economic standpoint of ergs, man-hours, and take-to-the-saloon pay, I was remunerated at the rate of one hundred dollars per word.

Therefore, until sworn testimony is offered to the contrary, I am pleased to report that the world championship is in the hands of an American — where it belongs. And I don't mean John O'Hara.

EARLY ON A May morning in 1927 Charles A. Lindbergh, push-ing eastward over the Atlantic in one of the greatest air adven-tures of history, saw a fishing boat below him and, being un-certain about his location, dipped his plane and roared down as close to the vessel as was prudent. He was only a few yards away when he yelled to the fishermen: "Which way to Ireland?" Later he wrote of the incident: "They just stared. Maybe they didn't hear me. Maybe I didn't hear them. Or maybe they thought I was just a crazy fool."

In my opinion Lindbergh was fortunate. If those fishermen were anything at all like people I encounter from day to day, and if they had signaled directions to him, he would probably have landed in Iceland, or the Azores, or Fort Lauderdale, Florida.

For all the other qualities of mind they may possess, the gen-erality of people, male and female, cannot properly direct a motorist or a pedestrian (or a Lindbergh in an airplane) to his destination; language seems to fail them at such moments. This is one of several reasons why I have given up long-distance auto touring. The clumsy, besnarled, ambiguous, equivocal, and mystifying information that lurks around every bend in the highway is almost more than Smith flesh can bare. And for re-lated reasons I shy away from invitations to the homes of people who live deeper in the country than I do. Most of them are un-able to tell me, clearly and succinctly, how to get to their houses. Many of them become certified lunatics whenever they undertake to give me a set of directions.

Several years ago my wife and I were invited to visit some

friends in rural Connecticut. I telephoned the lady of the house and asked for precise directions. She started off with simple and understandable sentences, but once she got me off the Merritt Parkway she lost me. Irretrievably. The one portion of her monologue that I remember most vividly went this way:

"You keep going quite a ways and finally you'll come to a big three-story gray house that is burned down and then . . ."

The stumbling block in that sentence would appear to be the big gray house that is burned down, but there is an equally insidious grammatical monstrosity — the phrase "quite a ways." There could be a difference of forty miles between what she considers to be quite a ways and what I consider to be quite a ways. How am I to know what a farmer means when he says the next town is a fur piece off? Or not very fur? Or jist beyant the next crossroads?

This ineptitude at direction-giving appears to be general among all the peoples of the world. The citizens of London are famous for their courtesy toward visitors who ask for directions; quite often a Londoner will abandon his own affairs and walk along with the tourist to the place he is seeking. Yet, in the storied countryside of Britain, there is never an end to the business of asking directions. You inquire of an English countryman how to get to Popskull-on-the-Rilleragh and he might respond as follows: "Proceed stryte ahead to the second roundabout and take the turning to the right and soon you will arrive at a cluster of small shops. Stop there, sir, and ask agayne." So you stop at the cluster of small shops and ask agayne and they send you along another few miles, advising you to stop at a certain tavern and . . . ask agayne.

In Italy and other countries which feature the Romance languages it is well to allow a certain time-lag; an Italian, giving directions, is capable of delivering a speech that would serve in accepting a Nobel prize.

In South Africa a motorist should never frame his question:

95

"Is this the way to Pretoria?" The answer will invariably be yes, even though he is heading straight for Nairobi and Addis Ababa. The proper way to put the question is: "Which way is it to Pretoria?" Thus stated, the question might possibly evoke a sensible answer. In Mexico and other Latin American countries every destination is *just beyond the next hill, señor.* The *beyond* involved here might well turn out to be twenty or eighty or a hundred and forty miles.

In the vast sprawl of Los Angeles there is not much point in asking directions. Nobody knows anything. People don't even know where they live. The Los Angeles taxi driver spends more time at the side of the road, wrestling with those crazy street maps, than he spends in transit. And if you are walking in Los Angeles and find it necessary to ask another pedestrian for directions, it is advisable to say, "Please don't talk — just point."

I know a young lady from overseas who recently took up residence in New York City. She tells me that she customarily asks six different people to direct her to her destination. "It is necessary," she explains, "to keep asking until you find two people in agreement. Then you can feel halfway certain. Out of six people you will find that two are dead wrong, two are right, and the remaining two will say, 'I'm sorry, but I'm a stranger here myself.' "

You're not really worse confounded, however, until you get to our new state, Hawaii. There the people employ a daffy language, Polynesian in origin, to indicate directions. They tell you to go *ewa* which usually means west, or *waikiki,* which often means east, or *mauka,* toward the mountains, or *makai,* in the direction of the sea. The people of Hawaii have a rather lame explanation for this terminology; they say that the customary directional terms, such as north and south, are not adequate on an island. It is my impression that they work on Nantucket and Long Island and Puerto Rico, but then maybe things are more delicately confused in the Pacific — possibly the International Date Line has something to do with it.

The chief fault of the average direction-giver is garrulousness, and overdevotion to detail. Sometimes it's merely a matter of loneliness — they just want to visit for a spell. Many people insist upon interpolating a lot of landmarks that only serve to bewilder the motorist. "Go straight out Gutteridge," a lady in Los Angeles told me recently, "and finally you'll come to Division Street. Cross Division, stay right on Gutteridge, just keep going out Gutteridge. After a while you'll come to Killjoy. Cross it, cross Killjoy, keep going, stay on Gutteridge, you'll see a big cemetery on a hill, then you'll come to a light, that'll be Cumshaw Boulevard. Cross Cumshaw, stay right on Gutteridge, go past a big supermarket with a red tower, just keep on going . . ." All of this drivel about cemeteries and Cumshaws and supermarkets and Killjoys could have been covered in one three-word sentence: "Stay on Gutteridge." As it was, I got fouled up somewhere along the way and ended up in Oxnard.

Then there is the person, usually a male creature proud of his efficiency, who showers you with fractions. "Turn right at the second traffic light," he says, "and go seven and eight-tenths of a mile to Hardscrabble Road, turn left, go three and three-tenths of a mile to Douglas, turn left, our house is exactly six and one-tenth miles from the intersection." I always feel a little let down that he doesn't tell me that I must go one-twentieth of a mile up his driveway to arrive at his back turnaround. I suppose this sort of precise detail is all right, though it's likely to be the death of me. I've come within one and one-fourth inches of annihilation through keeping my attention fastened on the mileage dial rather than the road.

Everyone has encountered the tangent-talker in the act of giving directions. Fearlessly, with no regard for possible consequences, I charge women with being the chief tangent-talkers.

I have heard a neighbor lady talking to a friend in the city, giving her directions, as follows: ". . . and then you come to this slate-gray house — no, it's more of a beige — it's a real nice house, cost fifty thousand if it cost a penny, but Susan, the people who live in it are the most hideous human beings, the most hateful people on earth, they have this monster of a dog, I think it's a Great Dane, but first let me tell you about her!" Then five solid minutes of pure gossip, with all thought of highway directions forgotten.

Many stories having to do with direction-giving involve a farmer, possibly with a straw in his mouth. I've heard of such a rustic who gave a motorist some complicated directions to get to a fishing resort. The motorist followed the instructions carefully, making all the prescribed turns, and wound up in front of the farmer again. He started to protest, but the farmer held up his hand. "Now," he said, "don't go blowin' a gasket. I just wanted to see if you know how to foller directions. 'Pears you do, so now I'll get you to the fishin' grounds."

One of the classic stories concerns the tourist who went astray in backwoods New England. He came at last to a dour Yankee.

"Where does this road go?" he asked.

"Ain't never seed it go nowheres."

"Well, how far is it to the next town?"

"Don't know — never measured it."

"You're not very smart, are you?"

"Maybe not — but *I* ain't lost."

A woman I know was driving to the Pacific Coast and in Iowa stopped to ask a farmer how to get to a certain town. He gave her a long routine of turn rights and bear lefts and finished off by saying, "You can't help but miss it."

There is a type of direction-giver who might be called the critic-editorialist. You stop and ask him how to get to the Bijou movie theater and he might respond: "You'll be making a mistake if you go there — the picture this week is lousy. Better wait till next week — they got Kim Novak coming in." Or, if you're trying to find the place where they're having the flower show, he'll advise you not to go — the woman who's running it is a stinker.

Consider, too, the highway engineer type. He describes each road and each section of road by the character of its surfacing. "You go three miles on this paving block till you hit ferrocrete," he says. "Turn left on the ferrocrete, go four miles and turn right on a tar job gritted with chippings, then two and a half miles to a fork, taking the grouted macadam instead of the bituminous clinker — the one with the steep cambers — and finally you'll come to a washboard bearing left . . ." This man baffles most of us, but no more so than the rural nature boy who instructs the driver from the city to "keep going till you come to a grove of hemlocks and then . . ." The city driver wouldn't know a grove of hemlocks from a pride of lions or a hand of bananas. Still, he would never confess that ignorance and so he probably ends up in a penetrable wilderness of hemlocks.

This brings us to that peculiar twist in the character of many men which forbids their ever asking directions of strangers. They will make inquiries in a filling station, but they refuse to stop along the highway and ask. This willful stubbornness has long been a source of provocation among husbands and wives, because wives believe in stopping and asking. "Stop and ask somebody," they'll say to a husband who is hopelessly lost, but he responds by setting his jaw and pushing on, deeper into the hot pampas or frozen tundra. I understand his attitude. I simply cannot conceive of a male creature whose lack of masculine pride would permit him to stop his car and, in effect, inform a dim-witted stranger that he is incapable of finding his destination without help. I, for one, will never do it. Robert Benchley once considered this problem and undertook to explain the psychology of the wife. Her insistence that her husband stop and

My husband!

99

ask directions is based on experience, said Benchley, "which has taught her that *any* one, no matter who, knows more about things in general than her husband."

I have heard of a man whose business takes him by car all over the country and who would prefer death in a deep canyon to asking a stranger for directions. This man drives into a strange town where he has a business engagement, finds a taxi and says to the driver, "Go to 1564 Hickory Street." Then he simply trails along after the cab.

There remains the matter of the wife-navigator on motor trips. In a Maryland motel I once met a professor who said: "As a general thing, it's always a bad idea for a man to ask his wife anything at all involving directions, especially if a road map is involved. The average woman has no sense of geography. A man visualizes, say, the state of Florida as it looks on the map; a woman thinks only of palm trees and beaches. She has no instinct for directions and certainly no understanding of maps."

Hogwash

This professor said that his own wife possessed an exceptional mind, played a good game of chess, knew all about the insides of guided missiles, and understood the writings of Gertrude Stein, yet she was thoroughly bewildered whenever she tried to read a map. Once they were twisting and turning their way through a town in North Carolina, following the highway signs, and she was studying the road map. Suddenly she cried out that they were off the track — the map showed the highway as going *straight through the town* without a single turn.

I have a female relative who confuses her husband by calling out distances in inches instead of miles. He'll ask her to look on the map and tell her how far they are from Decatur. Pretty soon she'll announce, "Exactly an inch and a half." After trying to cure her without success, this poor man had to learn to gauge map distances by inch rather than by mile.

My own wife has to turn the map and aim the road in the direction we're going, otherwise she wouldn't be able to tell a

100

right turn from a left turn. My favorite story of her navigational skill concerns the time we were driving west out of Indianapolis, headed for St. Louis. She was studying the map and suddenly she cried out, "What luck! There's a beautiful road, looks like a superhighway, that runs straight to Chicago — we can get on it at a town called Dana." I couldn't make out what she was talking about so I pulled over to the side and had her show me this superhighway. It was the state line between Indiana and Illinois. And the splendid point to her error was this: we were not even going to Chicago.

In the art of direction-giving I would naturally like to point to myself as a paragon of efficiency. I know how it should be done. If you live in a difficult locality and find it necessary to tell people on the phone how to get to your place, sit down and rehearse your speech. Make it simple, and make it crystal-clear. Don't clutter it up with cemeteries. Don't get off on tangents involving beige houses containing hideous people or three-story gray houses that are burned down. Don't confuse people with grouted macadam or cross streets called Killjoy or volleys of fractions. By all means take care with your terminology. And if you are precise instead of rambling, it may be that your guests will make it to your house, rather than end up face downward in the Hudson River six and three-tenths miles above Albany. Near a grove of hemlocks.

17. A STICKEN TO CHEW

RICHARD BISSELL wrote a novel. It became a best-seller and Broadway got interested in it. Mr. Bissell helped convert the novel into a musical comedy. The show was a huge success. So

Mr. Bissell wrote himself another novel. It hit the best-seller lists. It was about a fellow who wrote a novel and how the novel was converted into a musical comedy, and all the crazy things that happened in the process. This novel hit the best-seller lists. So Mr. Bissell and some other people made a musical comedy out of it, and the show was a big Broadway hit. Mr. Bissell has written still another novel and it will be turned into a musical comedy about a fellow who wrote a novel and had it turned into a musical comedy and then wrote a novel about a fellow who wrote a novel that was turned into a musical comedy, and *that* novel was turned into a musical comedy, and so the fellow says to his wife, I think I got a perty good thing agoin' and I better haul off and write me another novel.

Mr. Bissell is a friend of mine and for all his fantastic success at the typewriter I do not envy him. I hate him.

In a somewhat different form this progressive enrichment has happened to me. But in my case it has been no crude, tedious piling up of filthy money. Once I wrote a magazine article about malapropisms and spoonerisms. Readers began mailing in additional examples of syntactical confusion, and so I wrote another magazine article, and now the mail began to really pile in, so I wrote a third magazine article, and as you may have noticed I've used some of this wonderful material in this book, and there will be some more, and Mr. Richard Bissell can go soak his head. In the Mississippi River.

I still get a steady dribble of mail containing malapropisms and spoonerisms. People all over the land are talking upside down and backwards. I hear about them through correspondence and my ear is now tuned to the spasmodic spoonerisms of the television performers and the malapropisms of grocery clerk and insurance agent and week-end guest. And just to complicate matters, a kind of lunatic locution known as the Irish bull seems to be flourishing. I intend to discuss it, with samplings, later in this book (which will *not* be converted into a musical comedy).

Let us then continue a bit in those fields we have been exploring. In the matter of splendid solecisms I have recently heard a baseball telecaster say that Hank Bauer "reached safe firstly on a fielder's choice."

A relative of mine told me how she had once beaten the victim of a pockpicket. Frank Blair spoke of a Soviet diplomat who was "accompanied by several bardy gods." And, glory be, I heard a man on television talking about how he had been given a shot of penicillin, and he made mention of the doctor's "hypodcemic nerdle."

The mail indicates that people from West Quoddy Head in Maine to Point Arena in California are sputtering malapropisms and scattering spoonerisms over the landscape as never before in the history of the subordinate clause. One of the mail spoonerisms is concerned with the staff of life. In Kansas a radio announcer, delivering a spiel for a local bakery, declared that "bed breaking has been going on for centuries."

It appears that spoonerisms flourish best among radio and TV announcers, and among women doing business in the food marts. I have cross-examined several grocers of my acquaintance and found that they have preserved some fine examples of foodstuff spoonerisms. They remind me of the time when I was a child and one of my sisters said we were going to have "sopato poop" for lunch. The housewives of my neighborhood have at various times asked for jineapple poose, rot poast, craham gackers, roast bibs of reef and cream of sushroom moop. A really high-class job of grocery store spoonerizing was "sawlry celt." And one grocer told me of a telephone order in which the customer asked for a jar of "beet swazzle." He finally figured it out: sweet basil.

Previously we spoke of a lady who ordered "half a dozen

103

chork pops." Now comes V. Barnett, who takes oath that a lady out in Coos Bay, Oregon, went into a restaurant and asked for "smorked poke chops."

Mrs. Phyllis Gronseth of Albuquerque says her young daughter begged for money to buy gubble bum, while Mrs. Gronseth's aunt once remarked, "That's more truth than poultry."

In her teaching days, Mrs. D. J. Carson of Elizabethtown, Indiana, presided at a graduation ceremony and when it was over she addressed the audience, "Thank you for your presence and attention. This conclouds the poogrim." Mrs. Carson said she wasn't even aware of what she had said until someone told her about it later.

Mrs. W. L. Hille of New Orleans tells me that after she read one of my magazine pieces she felt superior to all those bunglers and flubbers, and then she went out to the butcher's and in a loud and firm voice announced that she wanted "a sticken to chew." Mrs. Ellis Blockson of Sewickley, Pennsylvania, reports that she heard an announcer introduce the song "Apple Blossom Time" as "Assel Bottom Time."

Helen MacKenzie of Elyria, Ohio, recalls someone mentioning Victor Hugo's book *The Soilers of the Tea.* And I've been told about a very proper lady from the South who, in a talk to members of a very proper literary club in New Jersey, committed a frightful but hilarious spoonerism when she spoke of Dickens' novel *A Sale of Two Titties.* I have no way of knowing how embarrassed she was over this blunder. Maybe not much. Some of the ladies have sent me spoonerisms more breath-taking than the Dickens book title. One housewife informed me that her husband had all his shirts made to order. One day the pastor of their church arrived at the house and said he wanted to see the husband. The wife said, "Oh, I'm sorry, he's downtown getting fitted for a shirt." Except that it came out spoonerized, sharply and distinctly. I assume she was embarrassed, but she didn't say so.

Veronica Denner of Obernburg, New York, reports that someone in her family once spoke of a "roam-fubber cushion" and the expression roam-fubber is now standard in her home. And Mrs. Gladys N. Robbins of Richmond, Indiana, confused a vacuum cleaner salesman one day by telling him: "I already hoove a Havver." Mrs. Robbins adds that her daughter came in from sledding and complained, "Mother, my froze are toe-sin." Mrs. Robbins has herself been guilty on occasion and once reported to her husband that she had been given a ticket for "expeeding the seed limit." In the field of malapropisms, she mentions a friend who is always hitting the head on the nail and sending packages by partial post.

Marion Maurer of New Haven is a collecter of both mala-propisms and spoonerisms and sends us a batch of each. Many of them came from the lips of a woman friend, including "I'll pit-hinch for her," and "We have a new ping-tong pable," and "I'm not going to mince berds" (which properly, should be "wince merds"). As for malapropisms, the same lady has com-mitted the following:

"We had some muled cider, flavored with old spice."

"I will *not* be bomineered!"

"She had a sore under her fingernail cubicle."

"That's all water under the dam."

"I get so mad I have to blow off stream."

"He had a flexigle spine, but very tight hamsprings." (The Lord alone knows the meaning of that one.)

There have been many other malapropisms in the mail and I have learned something new — that another name for a mala-propism is a "slipslop." The word comes from a character in a Fielding novel, a Mrs. Slipslop, who often and ludicrously misused one word after another. I remember a newspaper col-league in Denver, years ago, whose education was elementary, and who one day had to meet a train bringing a prominent movie actress to town. She stepped out of her Pullman car in a somewhat disheveled state and when the reporter returned to the office, his comment was, "Boy, was she bed-raggled!" That, to my mind, is a slipslop.

Mrs. Gladys P. Procter of Gloucester, Massachusetts, heard someone say, "Have you seen the pictures she took with her polio camera?" Mrs. Procter also reports on a woman who remarked, "Her hobby is bird-washing."

My neighbor Fels Hecht tells about a quite proper lady of his acquaintance who, on being complimented about her new shoes, said, "Yes, they are very comfortable — they make street walking a pleasure."

From Helen S. Bacon of Kansas City comes word of a student in a small-town Missouri high school who, in a moving recitation of "Thanatopsis," declaimed: "Like one that wraps the drapery of his crotch about him, and lies down to pleasant dreams."

I have word of people who have spoken of "an inferioppity complex" and who have said, "That's none-sense," and, in reference to an official known as a Sectional Emergency Coordinator "Ladies and gentlemen, I take pleasure in introducing our Sexual Emergency Coordinator." Those two words often get interchanged, as in the case of the colored woman who went into a North Carolina furniture store and said she wanted to buy a sexual sofa. The salesman managed to suppress a smile and then said he didn't quite understand what she meant. She then explained, "I just want an occasional piece in the living room."

Helen Lanier, who operates a beauty shop in Providence, has been collecting conversational bobbles for several years. She recalls one customer who had been to New York to see a play "with Walter Selzniak in it." Another was worried that her throat was becoming "creepy." The same lady said she wanted her hair to grow out so she could wear a "chigon." And still another said she had been terribly "rejected" lately on account of her "bronical trouble." A lady customer once said to Miss

106

Lanier, "Really, my dear, you are quite nave." And another said, "Oh, that's a lot of poppyrock." Miss Lanier once employed a male hairdresser who was somewhat less than intellectual. Shortly after he came to work for her, he hung two photographs of a woman on the wall. Under one photograph was the caption. "How Come." Under the other, "How Left." Miss Lanier asked him what on earth it all meant. "In this one" he said, "is how she come in, and in this one, how she went out." It was his way of saying "before and after."

A high school principal in Mississippi has written that he was so nervous on his first teaching job that he said to his pupils, "Those at your books close your seats." And he tells of an elderly female relative who, when asked where her daughter was, replied, "Oh, she's at home in the arms of Murphy."

Once I was telling Tommy Matson about a wild adventure I had recently enjoyed in a Manhattan saloon full of B-girls, and Tommy came up with a lovely coinage: "What were *you* doing in that din of inequity?"

There exists in our land a character whose job is to describe wrestling matches on television and whose wisdom I sometimes question. Once he was doing a tag-team match and the two filthy bums of the dirty team were having a whispered conference in their corner. "Let me tell you," cried the announcer, "there's some real deep skull-buggery going on up there!" This same man always says "pantomine" for pantomime, as do many other people I know, including the great patomime artist Red Skelton. And the wrestling announcer always says, in describing a keepsake or souvenir, that it is a lovely "momento." I have personally heard one of our leading American philosophers, Dave Garroway, say "momento" during a brief period on his show when he wasn't playing with toys.

I would enjoy having access to all the malapropisms committed by Yogi Berra. Some of them have been reported by Tom Meany, including, "Bill Dickey is learnin' me all his experience," and the one he spoke into the microphone on Yogi Berra Night at the Stadium: "I wanna thank you folks for makin' this night *necessary.*" Meany tells of the time Yogi was introduced to Ernest Hemingway and after the famous writer departed, Yogi said, "Quite a character. What's he do?" "He's a writer," gasped his companion. "Yeah?" said Yogi. "What paper?"

I'm happy to pass along the story of the Westchester matron who was shopping on a busy Saturday afternoon, and who was unable to find a place to park. She came bustling into Gristede's, hurried up to the meat counter, jostled several other customers to one side, and called out to the butcher, "Can you please wait on me now? I'm double-breasted!"

And finally, an item dating back to the time of O. O. McIntyre. The top Broadway columnist of Neanderthal times once reported that he had seen a woman get slammed around in a revolving door. She had just entered when a man in a hurry gave the door a hard shove, catapulting her into the lobby, and a moment later when she stood face to face with the offending party, she cried out: "Who do you push I am if a taxpayer is all I hope!"

I can't make out whether that's a malapropism, a spoonerism, or a line from the immortal works of Gertrude Stein.

❦❦❦❦❦❦❦❦❦❦❦❦❦❦❦❦❦❦❦❦❦❦❦❦

18. QUOTE UNQUOTE

No WRITER is worth his salt unless he engages himself in an occasional crusade for the good of mankind. Franklin P. Adams, in the years when he was running "The Conning Tower" column, bellowed almost constantly against the misuse of "who" and "whom" and he also complained bitterly about the inadequacy of house numbers in Manhattan. Lucius Beebe, during his term as a columnist in New York, howled in baroque language against those pedestrians who bear to the left on city sidewalks when, as he said, any civilized person knows that it is proper and orderly to walk always on the right. Those two men got pleasure from their crusades, though it is worth remark that multitudes still say "who" for "whom," that house numbers in Manhattan are inadequate, and that more people bear left on the sidewalks than ever before in history.

My own crusades have been just as mighty and grandiose as those of Mr. Adams and Mr. Beebe. Of late years I have concentrated my fire against the practice of attributing famous sayings to the wrong people. The most offensive example, which appears with appalling regularity in the public prints, always pinned on Mark Twain, is the line "Everybody talks about the weather, but nobody does anything about it." All available evidence indicates that this sentence originated with Charles Dudley Warner, who was a close friend of Twain's and who collaborated with the great humorist on the novel *The Gilded Age*. Warner, incidentally, also originated the phrase "Politics makes strange bedfellows." And *that* line is usually credited to a man named John Spencer Bassett, author of a biography of Andrew Jackson. I really bleed for poor Charles Dudley Warner. Posterity has not been nice to him.

A single week seldom goes by that I don't see the weather remark in print or hear it spoken on television or radio, and always and invariably it is attributed to Mark Twain. He doesn't need it. He wrote a million or so excruciatingly funny lines in his lifetime and his reputation won't collapse if credit for the weather quip is accorded another man. I actually cringe whenever I see it in print or hear it spoken. But it will not be put down. I have written to newspaper editors and columnists and magazine people and broadcasters but they pay no attention to me and the thing shows up more than ever, even appearing frequently in advertisements. It is, to use the phrase commonly attributed to Samuel Goldwyn, "a terrible carriage of misjustice." (Mr. Goldwyn never said it.)

The second quotation which arouses my hackles is the line "Go West, young man." It is variously rendered in that four-word version, also as "Go West, young man, go West," and again as "Go West, young man, and grow up with the country." It is always attributed to Horace Greeley. This error prevails in the town where I live, which is the town where Horace Greeley made his home for many years. His statue stands here, a couple of his houses are still occupied, the main street is Greeley Avenue, the high school is named for him, and the people of the town frequently say, "Well, as old Horace put it, go West, young man." The injunction actually had its origin in an article written by John B. L. Soule in the Terre Haute *Express* in 1851. Greeley, then editor of the New York *Tribune,* quoted it in one of his editorials. Immediately people started using the phrase and crediting Greeley with it. He disclaimed authorship, loudly and publicly, again and again, and finally tried to set matters straight by reprinting Soule's complete article. Whenever I see it in print or hear it on the air I write to the party in error, but it seems to be a hopeless crusade. The public is convinced that Horace Greeley said it. His name, in fact, has become an essential part of the quotation, just as Mark Twain's name has become an essential part of the weather remark. Most people, if they think of Horace Greeley at all, remember him only for go-West, disregarding the fact that he was the greatest single journalistic influence in the nation for more than thirty years, and once ran for the Presidency.

There are many popular quotations often credited to the wrong people. It is unlikely, for example, that Louis XIV ever said, "I am the State." It is unlikely for the simple reason that Louis *wasn't* the State, and had real rough going with the

110

French *parlements*. Scholars have proved quite conclusively that Voltaire never said or wrote, "I disapprove of what you say, but I will defend to the death your right to say it." What he actually wrote was, "Think for yourselves and let others enjoy the privilege to do so." There is a considerable difference between the two versions. The more popular, often-quoted line was made up by a lady who edited Voltaire's letters; she thought the master iconoclast's own phrasing lacked "punch." I am not a violent man, but I would enjoy shooting her down with a hackbut.

"Let them eat cake," attributed always to Marie Antoinette, appeared in the writings of Rousseau when Marie was eleven years old and not yet a resident of France. And both John Donne and Lord Byron spoke of "blood, sweat and tears" before Winston Churchill was ever born. But these errors belong to Europe and I'm inclined to let European crusaders fight to rectify them. There is enough for me to do on this side of the ocean.

In the last year another disheartening error in the field of quotation has been swiftly gaining ground. It involves the authorship of the line, "Any man who hates dogs and little children can't be *all* bad." I have seen it in print at least half a dozen times and each time it has been attributed to the late W. C. Fields. Just recently it has been quoted as a Fields saying in a leading literary magazine and at about the same time it was attributed to Fields by a critic on the staff of our most sophisticated weekly periodical. I think that there is a chance that I can knock it in the head and restore credit to the man who actually uttered it. I am sure of my ground here because W. C. Fields told me himself that the words were spoken by Leo Rosten at a testimonial dinner in 1939. Mr. Rosten is an author, a teacher, and a scholar. His employment of the "dogs and little children" line at the Fields dinner was reported accurately by the Associated Press and quoted in *Time*. And

111

just to set the record straight, I offer my own version of the affair as reported in one of my early books. It follows:

They gave a dinner not so long ago to honor W. C. Fields for having finished out forty years in show business. The speakers started speaking in the middle of the green beans and the gooey sentiment was passed around in washtubs. Orators such as Eddie Cantor and George Jessel stood up and talked and let the tears flow down their cheeks until it was almost necessary to club them to the floor in order to stop them . . . There were other recitations long and dull, and it was coming along toward two or three o'clock in the morning. The newspapermen were fidgeting and squirming and yawning and now and then gulping water to avoid heaving up their leg of lamb with mint sauce.

At last the toastmaster struggled to his feet. Everyone uttered a quiet prayer, hopeful that this time he would dismiss the class. He didn't.

"And now," he said, "just one more speaker and we'll call it a night. It is my pleasure, gentlemen, to present you with Dr. Leo C. Rosten, who has a few remarks."

The newspapermen groaned. A doctor yet! Probably a professor ready to give a paper on "The Anatomy of the Belly Laugh." Dr. Rosten was not known to them at that time as the genius who, among other brilliant achievements, had given the world the incomparable H*Y*M*A*N K*A*P*L*A*N.

He stood up and said:

"It is my opinion that any man who hates dogs and little children can't be *all* bad."

Then he sat down, and the newspapermen emerged from their torpor and cheered him as if he had just announced the death of Hitler.

There it is. I wrote it and so you can accept it as gospel. I think it is utterly ridiculous for people to credit it to Fields. So please, writers and broadcasters of America, *please* let me win just this one crusade! W. C. Fields, too, uttered many a memorable line and if he were alive today he would never claim authorship of this one. I think, perhaps, that he'd more likely take pride in the line he originated in *My Little Chickadee*

112

when, disgusted with the conduct of a bothersome Indian, he snarled, "Why don't you go back to your reservation and milk your elk?"

At least I *think* he originated it.

THE TIME has now come for me to reveal to the world why I have never cultivated a mustache. I'm sure a mustache would enhance my distinguished looks and that it would cause women to whicker as I passed along the boulevard. But I can't risk it, because even a little mustache is a dangerous thing. It invites comment.

If, wearing a mustache, I found myself in the company of the rougher and ruder elements of our society (meaning the people with whom I habitually associate), I would be exposed to uncomplimentary language, such as, "You been chewing on a moose?" I could take that sort of thing with good grace. The serious trouble would come from better-bred people. They are always searching for an excuse to pass a compliment, and a mustache, looming there in the middle of the face, is an open invitation. If a lady came up to me and said, "You have the most charming mustache I have seen in years," I wouldn't know how to respond. I might be thrown into such a panic that I'd blurt out, "I like yours, too."

One of the greatest paradoxes to be found in social intercourse is this: It is much easier to respond to an insult than it is to a compliment; we live in a talky world and whole legions of learned men have furnished us with rules for improving the art of polite conversation; yet we seem to suffer a shortage of people who can instruct us in the diplomacy of chitchat. That's where most of us get into trouble, in the area of small talk where we flub and fumble and embrace the *faux pas*. This is the home area of the compliment because, like it or not, the compliment is all too often a mere conversational device, ranking second only to the weather as an instrument for stirring up talk. Yet there are many of us who react to a compliment as if it were a mallet-blow on the head. Someone utters a pleasing, praiseful remark in our direction and we grow inarticulate and our kneecaps begin to vibrate.

"The sweetest of all sounds is praise," wrote Xenophon. Still, few of us can harken to those sweet sounds and retain our equanimity and aplomb. I don't like to quote a Greek without also quoting a Roman; it was Seneca who said: "You can tell the character of every man by the way in which he receives praise." Seneca was a philosopher and therefore we've got to believe whatever he said, even though it makes us unhappy. Seneca makes *me* unhappy. If people are able to read my character by the manner in which I react to a compliment, I'm certain that they put me down as a person who would abscond with funds.

I can't even accept, with grace, a compliment mistakenly bestowed upon me for a thing that isn't mine. It happens that I live on a hill overlooking a wide valley. Visitors at my house almost invariably exclaim: "My! What a terrific view you have here!" There it lays out there, the whole valley. I didn't do it. It was there long before I arrived on earth. It doesn't belong to me. Yet I always respond with a sickly smirk and say, "Oh, it isn't really much — just a lot of old real estate." Or I disparage its true quality by saying, "It may *look* like a nice view, but it's really all full of unpleasant people and the school taxes would gag a mule." The nearest I ever came to downright acceptance of this particular compliment was the time I responded with,

114

"Well, *we* like it." I employed that response even though it is a statement that has always mystified me. To say of a thing, "Well, *we* like it," is to imply that a lot of other people think it reeks. Not long ago I was in a group which included a geophysicist from Australia. He was talking quite eloquently about the wonders of the universe and he said: "This world you live on — this great, vibrant, spinning earth of yours — is a congeries of incredible marvels." There was a long pause and then a lady sitting opposite him, carried away by the vastness of his complimentary remark, said, "Well, *we* like it."

I think we make a mistake when we react to a compliment with denial and derogation. "What a stunning gown!" your friend says. "Oh, this old rag!" you respond. The situation here, incidentally, is almost exactly the same as the situation regarding the view from my front yard. You have no right to bridle and blush over any praise directed at your gown — unless it happened that you stitched it up yourself. The people who designed it, the people who manufactured it, even the man who herded the sheep which furnished the wool — they are more entitled to the compliment than you. You would be better off if you'd just say something like, "I had to fist-fight another woman in Macy's basement to get possession of it." Or better yet, "My husband picked it out for me."

It is apparent that some people have recognized the problem involved in responding to compliments, but not many of them have found an adequate solution. I know a married couple in New York who quite obviously have put their minds to it and decided on a technique for brushing off praise. They employ a sort of unreasonable realism. One evening I overheard a woman say to the husband, "What powerful shoulders you have!" Without blinking an eye he answered, "Three-fourths water. My body is three-fourths water, therefore my shoulders are three-fourths water and anything that's three-fourths water couldn't actually be very powerful." The well-intentioned woman went away with a furrowed brow and whispering to herself. And the wife of the man with the watery shoulders, when told that she has lovely skin, which she has, confuses everyone by responding, "It may look lovely to the naked eye, but it's really dead as a doornail. The outer layer of skin on the human body, no matter how nice it looks, is made up of dead cells." I don't think these two people are on the right track.

Courtliness of manner went out with the Welsbach mantle and today many of us try to answer a compliment with a quip or a witticism. "I've been hearing about you for years," someone says glowingly. "Nothing good, I hope," is the standard reply. A housewife might say, "Mr. Shobbly, I want to compliment you on the way you fixed that leaky faucet. You did a perfect job." And Mr. Shobbly replies, "I bet you say that to all the plumbers." This sort of thing, the witty retort, ought to be placed under government regulation. Maybe I'm appalled by it for the reason that somewhere in the world there is an epigram to fit every dilemma. If that be so, mine are all hidden under a rock in Southern Rhodesia, for I am never able to turn a compliment with a quip. I know of people who can do it, but for every genuinely clever retort there are a thousand that fall flat. It takes a Dorothy Parker or a George S. Kaufman or even a Charlie Chaplin to handle the quip-comeback with skill. When Elinor Glyn was introduced to Chaplin she wanted to say something complimentary, so she said, "You are not nearly as funny-looking as I thought you'd be." Said Chaplin: "Neither are you."

I would like to make mention of the special problem faced by artists, authors, and composers. When a new automobile or a new toothbrush comes off the assembly line, the people responsible for it are behaving properly when they call in outsiders and point to the product and swell out their chests and say, "Isn't she a beauty?" Not so a man who paints a picture or writes a book or composes a symphony. "That last sonnet

116

of yours, Ploffer," says the poet's friend, "that was a jim-dandy job, and it rhymed good." Ploffer, in his poetic heart, is in full agreement with this verdict but he can't say so. "Oh, really now," he protests, "You know very well that the cadence fell all apart in the sestet." Being the author of a whole stack of books I have on occasion been exposed to this situation. "That new book of yours," someone might say, "I found it very entertaining." It seems to me that I should be permitted to reply, "Well, I'm glad somebody liked it — I worked like a dog to get it written." Or, "I thought it was good, too, else I wouldn't have had it published." But no. The unwritten code of authorhood compels me to say, "You must be a person of execrable literary judgment."

In searching for a technique by which I might be able to cope with compliments, I have turned to the children. The very young children are of no help. Say to one of them, "My, what a fine little boy you are!" What does he do? He races across the room, flops to the floor, tries to stand on his head, leaps to his feet again, dashes around in circles, rolls his eyes in an alarming way, and rams his tongue out of the side of his mouth. I could do that sort of thing, but I don't think it would be accepted socially. Or try a compliment on a little girl. "What a *pretty* dress!" you exclaim. Instantly she heists it up to point out that her petticoat is even prettier, and then she heists the petticoat to show you that her panties are the prettiest of all. This sort of procedure would hardly work in adult society.

The older children are equally realistic, but they are inclined to make a business proposition out of a compliment. They originated and they habitually employ the time-honored device known as the T.L., or trade-last. "I got a T.L. for you," says one child to another. The second child then has to search his mind for some complimentary remark he has heard about the first, such as, "Well, Mary Willersknit told me you got beautiful ears." Only then will the first child come through with delivery of this T.L. It is a useful and admirable institution, the T.L., yet I cannot recommend it for general employment among grownups. As I remember the days of my tenderness, the T.L. can be and often is used as a devastating weapon. If I approached Mary Willersknit and told her that I had a T.L. for her she might put a studious look on her face, place her hand to her chin, paw the ground with her foot, scan the sky, scratch her head, and say, "Well, how, let . . . me . . . uh . . . see. Uh . . . let . . . me . . . think . . . now. Uh, uh, er, uh, uh, uh . . ." She acts as if she had never in all her years ever heard a nice thing said about me.

For a while I thought I might learn something from the Spanish-speaking people. They are the most adroit people on earth for mastery of the conversational amenities. They are exceptionally skilled at turning a compliment, and turn it they do. You say to one of them, "This is the most beautiful house I've ever been in." And they respond, "It is made immeasurably more beautiful by your lovely presence." You are left standing there with immeasurably lovely egg on your face. There would be no point in your trying to play the game back at them — it would sound foolish for you to continue with, "But the house is so much more beautiful than I could ever hope to be." They'd top you in the end, no matter what.

In considering this problem one thing is clear: the fact that poise lies at the bottom of all graceful social intercourse. Eliza W. Farrar, who wrote one of America's earliest books of etiquette, preached long and hard on the importance of poise. In illustration she told of an elegant New England dinner party at which the host was carving a goose. The bird got away from him, flew out of the dish, and landed in the lap of a lady of quality. Given the same circumstances I would have quietly asked for a coil of rope. This host, however, had poise. He said, with superb calmness and gravity, "Madam, I will thank you for that goose."

118

It is difficult to teach a natural-born bumbler how to be poised, but we might acquire a little bit of it if we keep one thing in mind. Whenever a person pays you a compliment, the chances are that he's just making conversation. I have a friend who, at every encounter, says to me, "You're looking exceptionally well." He says it on days when I'm pretty close to being a basketcase. The thing has reached the point where, if I hear him say that I'm looking exceptionally well, I'm swept from head to foot by a concatenation of aches and pains. They may be psychosomatic, but they hurt just as much as open wounds.

The whole thing makes me think of an Al Jolson story. Al was a raging hypochondriac and thereby a great boon to the medical profession. Once, one of his battery of doctors was making conversation by telling him of a certain rare disease.

"What makes this disease so odd," said the doctor, "is that the man who has it shows no outward sign of illness. In fact he has no sensation of sickness at all — he looks and feels as if he were in perfect, robust health."

"My God!" shrieked Jolson, clutching at his chest. "Those are *my* symptoms exactly!"

20. BIOGRAPHY OF A WORD

ALONG toward the end of 1950 a press association, devoting a small portion of its transmission time to the cultural aspects of contemporary living, carried an item from Hollywood proclaiming that a motion picture titled *Rhubarb* would soon go into production at Paramount. This item came to the attention of an association of rhubarb growers in Louisiana and an alert official of the organization sent off a letter *correo aereo* to Paramount, offering know-how cooperation, suggesting a promotional tie-in, and recommending that a qualified rhubarb grower be taken on as technical advisor.

Paramount, of course, had no use for a rhubarb grower because the picture had been envisioned without the employment of a single ratty stalk of *Rheum rhaponticum,* or common garden rhubarb. The film, in fact, would serve as convincing evidence that a new improper noun has become firmly embedded in the common speech of America. The word *rhubarb,* as it appears day after day in the American press, seldom has reference to pie filling. In its new identity, it has been defined in Supplement II of H. L. Mencken's *The American Language* as baseball slang for "an altercation on the field." It has long since outgrown that definition. A larger explanation (quoted by Mr. Mencken) is contained in a novel called *Rhubarb,* published in 1946 and written by me, using both hands. This second definition follows:

Then and there the cat got his name — perhaps the only printable name he ever had — derived from a colloquialism insinuated into the Yankee vernacular by Red Barber, the baseball broadcaster. Mr. Barber in turn picked it up from the prose writings of Gary Schumacher and spread it to the far-wandering winds. In Mr. Barber's lexicon a rhubarb was a noisy altercation, a broil, a violent emotional upheaval brought on by epical dispute — such as whether one grown man had touched another grown man on the body with a ball the size of a smallish orange.

The word as thus defined has advanced into wide general usage during the last few years. In 1951 I saw it used to describe a dispute which arose at a session of the United Nations, and it appeared in a dispatch from the Far East, where a rhubarb developed during the cease-fire talks at Kaesong. There are backstage rhubarbs today in opera, and a beat rhubarb among the literati. I've been informed, too, that the editorial committees which pass upon new words for our standard dictionaries are engaging in small rhubarbs themselves over the question of recognizing the newcomer.

So far as I can find out, the word has had but one previous incarnation in the lexicon of slang. Among British dockworkers a rhubarb was a loan, so denominated "because of its ruddy length." In my own experience I can recall another specialized use of the word. During the 1930's it was employed as a method of simulating crowd noises in radio broadcasts. Someone discovered that if the script called for the hum and buzz of conversation in a crowd, the effect could be best achieved by having everyone in the studio say, "Rhubarb and rhubarb and rhubarb and rhubarb . . ." Try it with a crowd and you'll get the effect of a mob working itself up to a tree-limb hangin'.*

The Rhubarb of the novel and the motion picture was a cat — an extraordinarily mean and supercilious and cantankerous cat, therefore lovable. Through inheritance this cat became the owner of a major-league baseball team. Inasmuch as the novel and, more particularly the movie, helped to solidify the word's acceptance, I would like to explain that I almost went to the well without it. When I started writing the book I wanted to give the cat a name out of baseball jargon, and most of the baseball jargon I knew had been acquired from the radio broadcasts of the aforementioned Red Barber. Mr. Barber, as noted earlier in this book, employed a variety of sassy locutions out of his Confederate background in describing the labors of the Brooklyn Dodgers. When a ball team was engaged in a wild and frenetic scoring rampage, he would sometimes say, "They're sure tearin' up the pea patch!" When I first began

* Know how to imitate a cocktail party? Get four people, two men and two women, into a room. Give each of them a book or a magazine. Have them pick any passage of prose—it doesn't make any difference what it is. Then, on signal, have all four begin to read *with feeling.* If people were in an adjoining room they'd swear they were listening to twenty or thirty jabbering party guests.

composing my inimitable vulgarities about the cat, I named him Peapatch. About halfway through the book, however, I grew dissatisfied with my hero's name — it sounded just a trifle too cute — and so I changed it to Rhubarb. Then when Paramount bought the picture rights to the book, I felt almost certain that they would change the name of the cat and the title of the story as a matter of policy. I was fully prepared to see my cat on the screen as Eggplant, or Okra, or Kohlrabi, or Gooseberry. But never once was any such change suggested.

The book itself had a wide circulation with the consequence that a great many people around the country began naming their own cats Rhubarb. One of these was a cat inhabiting a beer parlor in the neighborhood of Cornell University. The lady proprietor of this establishment not only named her cat Rhubarb, but had trained him to walk up and down the bar with a small stalk of garden rhubarb in his teeth. My own favorite among the real Rhubarbs, however, was an outsize tomcat belonging to a doctor in a small Missouri town. This Missouri Rhubarb could turn electric lights on and off by leaping at the wall switches, and he was a pool shark. The doctor had a pool table in his home. He would scatter the fifteen balls over the table, then say, "Your shot, Rhubarb." The cat would leap onto the table and, using both paws, swiftly pocket all fifteen balls. I have not seen him perform this feat, but I believe the story. If the doctor had told me that he pocketed the balls in rotation — beginning with the Number 1 ball and going on up to Number 15 — then I would have suspected that the doctor was lying. He made no such claim. The cat shot straight pool.

As to the etymology of rhubarb — it appears that there is a definite relationship between the two widely divergent meanings of the word. Let us take, first, the plant. It got its name from the Greek *rheon barbaron,* meaning something that comes from the barbarous country of the Rha (Volga) River. The plant has thick succulent petioles, and these petioles are loaded with chrysarobin, calcium oxalate, rheotannic acid, emodin, apor-rhetin, and mucilage. I have heard that the leaves are poison-ous and the rhubarb circulios, which are bugs, stay away from them, devoting their energies to boring holes in the petioles. The plant is susceptible to a disease called Phytopthora Foot which, strangely enough, is a form of crown rot. I know people who take down with it. Crown rot, I mean.

If I were a rhubarb grower — if my family fortune and fame derived from the cultivation of rhubarb — I believe that I would resent the new connotation of the word, and I might even launch a movement to change the name of my product al-together. Pieplant would do — in many sections of the United States rhubarb is generally addressed by that name. It is also called, in various localities, wine plant, apple-cabbage and ap-ple-peru. Along the Maine coast it is known as rhubub.

There is significance in the fact that rhubarb has for cen-turies occupied a prominent position in the world's pharma-copoeia. The dried rhizomes and roots of certain Chinese and Tibetan varieties have long been valued as a purgative and as a stomachic bitter. And the medicinal value of ordinary garden rhubarb has been known to generations of American mothers. Which brings us back to Garry Schumacher.

Mr. Schumacher spent many years as a baseball writer with the New York *Journal-American*. He is a native of the Green-point section of Brooklyn. He has informed me that when he was a boy, the mothers of Greenpoint held firmly to the belief that rhubarb was essential to the good health of their children, that seasonal dosages of rhubarb would invigorate them and permit them to fight like bobcats and thus get along in the world. In the Greenpoint springtimes of forty years ago every kid had a rhubarb routine to follow. The moment school was out, it was ordained that he go straight home, where his mother would hand him a slice of bread with a portion of stewed rhubarb smeared on it. Mr. Schumacher admits that, as of today, he considers rhubarb to be a near delicacy, but when he was a boy it bore the stigma of a medicament. It was good fuh ya, therefore it was revolting, and he and all his friends despised it as children of my own tender years despised castor oil.

They would scamper home then, after school, and get their rhubarb-smeared bread, then head at once for the street games that awaited them — street games that usually included whaling hell out of each other. The fighting sometimes started before the boys had finished off their rhubarb and it was not uncommon for a boy to find himself with rhubarb in his hair and down his neck and in his ears. In time, says Mr. Schumacher, the Greenpoint kids began referring to their happy play as rhubarbs — exclaiming through puffed lips, "Wotta rhubarb!"

Mr. Schumacher somehow grew up and the word disappeared into his subconscious and lay dormant there, like a rhubarb circulio with a bellyful of chrysarobin. Then one day around 1940 when he was assigned to chronicle the doings of the Brooklyn Dodgers, the Brooklyn manager, Leo Durocher, engaged in a particularly violent argument with an umpire, as was his custom. Dust was kicked, gloves were thrown, strong language flew, people were banished for inciting to riot . . . and that evening Mr. Schumacher was reflecting on the noble fury of the affair when the old Greenpoint cry rose out of his subconscious and he found himself exclaiming, "Wotta rhubarb!"

The phrase once resurrected stayed alive in his mind and he inserted it in his sports copy, and it appealed to Mr. Barber, who was sorely in need of a new word to describe the antics of the rhubarbing Dodgers and . . .

Mr. Barber now tells me that Tom Meany had something to do with jogging Mr. Schumacher's memory about the origin of the word, and a brawl in a saloon and a colorful bartender figure in it somewhere. I don't want to withhold any credit

124

from Mr. Meany, else we all might have a rhubarb on our hands, but if I get into that saloon story, we'll *never* get home for dinner.

21. *AMERICAN SPOKEN HERE*

THE ACTOR Cyril Ritchard tells a story of an overrefined English lady who, visiting in Italy and unable to communicate with the natives, finally complained: "I don't see why, if one speaks slowly and distinctly, English should not be understood by everybody."

There have been moments, in foreign climes, when I have had the same feeling. I know that in these days of simplified teaching methods it is considered boorish as well as unwise for an American to visit a foreign country without first learning a smattering of the language. Yet I am prepared to argue the matter. I say that if you are planning a trip to continental Europe or to Latin America and you have no knowledge whatever of any foreign tongue, and you don't have the time to do any studying, then leave it that way. You'll have just as much fun being dumb and hysterical. Maybe more.

In the first place there is no such thing as a smattering of French. If you are the type who insists on personal colloquy with the natives, there is only one course open to you: spend at least six months in assiduous study at home, then go to France and live among Frenchmen for a year; after that you are adequately prepared to go to France.

Personally I am convinced that no amount of schooling would ever get me to talking French and, as for German, I simply shut my eyes and try not to think about it. My friends say, "Oh, it's only in your mind." That's precisely what they say to me when I argue that I can't sleep at night if I drink coffee in the evening. "It's only in your mind," they say. Of course it's in my mind! That's the main part I sleep with, just as my mind is the part I use most in trying to speak French.

Perhaps that's my trouble. It may be that French is a thing you learn more with the roof of the mouth than with the brain. It is necessary to *manipulate* and *maneuver* the roof of the mouth, and I simply can't manage it. The roof of my mouth always seems to be stiff and untractable. I sometimes try to run a bluff by saying, "I can't speak French because I have a Middlewestern palate." I've even got so I *believe* that's the reason.

In Paris I finally acquired a few words of broken French, and I mastered the approximate pronunciation of *monsieur* but only because the Tobias brothers, twenty-some years earlier, wrote a popular song called "Miss You." Like many thousands of Americans before me I have always wanted to pronounce *monsieur* the way it is spelled, the way the doughboys of World War I are said to have pronounced it, i.e., mon-sewer. But in Paris, each time I had occasion to use the salutation, I compelled myself to remember the Tobias song and then spoke the title of it (sometimes I sort of sang it) and quite a few Frenchmen knew what I was saying. On at least one occasion I suffered a mental lapse and sang out, "Monsieur, since you went away dear."

In France, in Switzerland, and in Italy my unilingual wife and I had many fine adventures, but when we got home the things that stood out in memory, the things we wanted to tell about, were the language-block incidents.

Later, in Mexico, we did make an earnest effort to learn some Spanish, but the consequences were often ludicrous. For example, an incident in the city of Morelia. I had heard that in Mexico, if you are able to be polite in Spanish, you'll get by

126

handsomely. So we drilled ourselves in the phrases of courtesy, such as *por favor* and *gracias,* and I told my wife that she should employ these words in any and all circumstances. She was out marketing that day in Morelia when a Mexican gentleman, slightly intoxicated, approached her and made an improper proposal. My wife smiled at him politely and said, "No, *gracias, señor.*" He followed her, persisting in his suit, and she continued to respond with, "No, *muchas gracias, señor.*" The proper response, of course would have been to belt him one with her shopping bag.

I wrote of my wife's politeness in a book about Mexico. Later my friend Paul Perez of Oaxaca told me about a woman friend of his, from San Francisco, and how she had a similar experience with a Mexican gentleman in Mexico City. The Mexican approached her and made what was quite clearly an indecent (!) proposal. She knew a few words of Spanish which she had acquired from looking at western movies and television shows. She spoke sharply to the romantic Mexican, saying *"Vámonos!"* She believed the word to mean, "Begone! Scat! Hit the road!" But he did not hit the road. Instead he moved in closer and beseeched the tourist lady to indulge his passion. Again she told him to *vámonos,* but the command only served to increase his ardor, and he was about to seize her in his arms when she saw some other Yankee tourists up ahead. She hurried into their company, and the Mexican went his way, and she now explained the trouble she had undergone with him, and how he ignored her command to *vámonos.* Only then did she learn, as her fellow tourists informed her, than when she said *"Vámonos!"* she was saying, "Let's go!" or "Let's get going!"

In Paris one afternoon I "died" in the middle of the Boulevard St. Germain. We had been sopping up atmosphere at one of the sidewalk tables of the Café Deux Magots (just about as *unsavory* a name as anyone could think up for a restaurant).

I consulted the itinerary I had worked out at breakfast and found it was time for us to visit Napoleon's tomb. You'll get absolutely nowhere in France saying "Napoleon" the way we say it in America. I knew this already. I knew that the proper way to say it is "Nap-oley-onh." At least I thought I knew it.

We walked out into the middle of the boulevard where the taxicabs were stationed and approached one of the drivers.

"Nap-oley-onh," I told him with great confidence. I thought that would be sufficient, but the man just gave me a dumb, Gallic stare.

"Tomb . . . of . . . Napoley-onh," I said, employing the manner ordinarily used in speaking to tiny children. He began darting glances around the street as if looking for help. I took hold of his arm and said, commandingly, *"Attendez* moy." I put my right hand inside my jacket, shortened my stature by crouching at the knees, and said loudly and firmly, "Nap-oley-onh. Nap . . . oley . . . onh!" Now he fired a volley of grape-shot over my head, the tone of which indicated that he had no inkling of what I was talking about and, in fact, suspected that I was trying to borrow money from him.

"Nap-oley-onh!" I persisted. "Nap-oley-onh. Tomb. Die. Dead. Mort. Morty. Nap-oley-onh. Dead. Body. Dead body."

"You're attracting attention," said my wife. The people at the two sidewalk cafés were all staring at us, but I figured that most of them were Existentialists, loaded with van, so I didn't care. I was downright sore at the stupidity of this driver in the presence of such a simple statement as Nap-oley-onh. After all, if a Frenchman came up to me on the street in New York and said, "You lee siss as grand," I feel sure I'd have sense enough to direct him to the tomb of Ulysses S. Grant. So I kept at it, growing louder, and finally I made a pistol out of my hand, placing the index finger to my temple and waggling the thumb. I said "Bang!" and closed my eyes and jerked my head back and forth a couple of times in what I fancied was rather an expert portrayal of a man with a bullet through his brain. Then I began weaving and staggering slightly.

"You're giving tourists a bad name," my wife said. I ignored her and said, "Dead! Nap-oley-onh! Tomb!" I threw my head back, eyes closed, and crossed my arms over my chest and cried out, "Napoley-onh!"

That did it. "Walla!" cried the driver. "Onh-va-leed!" He seemed *so* happy that he had been unable to understand an American with so little difficulty. And he took us to The Invalides. My friends tell me that if I'd have said "Onh-va-leed" in the beginning, he'd have known. I doubt it, for I have a strong tendency to pronounce The Invalides as if it meant The Sick People.

My death scene on the Boulevard St. Germain was only one of many memorable incidents which made our continental journey more exciting than it would have been if we had known the language. Eventually we left Paris on an overnight train for Lugano in the southern part of Switzerland. We were going into a country where they speak *four* foreign languages, but people told us not to worry. "Everybody in Switzerland speaks English," they said. These same people told us, incidentally, that Swiss trains run like Swiss watches. I thought they ran remarkably like trains.

We were highballing through Switzerland when we got out of our berths the next morning and made our way to the restaurant car. We sat down at a table and I told my wife that I would do the ordering because I do not speak foreign languages better than she doesn't. The kitchen was right behind me, within a few feet of our table but hidden by a partition. There were perhaps a dozen other travelers in the car. Finally a waiter came up and said something to us in Italian and my wife said she thought she'd start with prunes.

"Prunes," I said to the waiter. He registered imbecility. He then delivered a long harangue in which, I believe, he was trying to establish if we spoke French, Italian, German, Romansch, Esperanto, Swahili, or Gregg shorthand. I answered him with one word. "Prunes," I said firmly. He repeated it to himself, mispronouncing it in some clever way, but I nodded and he went on into the kitchen. We could hear the conversation back there — two or three men talking explosively.

"Proooon!" they were saying. "Prooon? *Proooon?* PROON?"

After a while the waiter came back and talked some more in Italian, and shrugged a good deal, and from the way he kept saying "Prooon" I realized that he wasn't pleading lack of prunes, but lack of comprehension. Then I remembered having seen prunes on a menu in Paris, so now I got out a pencil and pad and printed the word *pruneau*. He studied it a while and I said "Prunes" several times more, and he went back to the kitchen.

I never heard such carrying on! Someone back there yelled, "Prooon-ah! Prooon-oh!" Someone else cried, "Ah-prooon!" And there was a great scurrying and scuffling and several minutes passed, and then our waiter emerged in triumph, and placed in front of my wife . . . one soft-boiled egg. She clutched at her throat and turned her head away, for she cannot even *witness* a soft-boiled egg first thing in the morning. She made waving motions, indicating that he should take the abomination out of her sight. He was crestfallen and as he picked it up I told him, softly, "Prunes."

Back in the kitchen there were sounds bordering on lamentation, and wondering cries of "Ah-prooon!" and "Prooon-ah!" and "Prooo-uns!" I realized that we were no closer to prunes than we had been when we boarded the train. I thought of trying to act out a prune — making a charade of it. At first a pantomime signifying prune seemed both ridiculous and impossible; then I thought of trimming limbs off trees and shrubbery, and made a few tentative motions as if I were operating a pair

130

of hedge-clippers. But I abandoned the idea, for fear he would fetch me a set of Cuban maracas, or two buggy whips.

I still had the pencil and pad on the table, so I made a quick sketch of a prune, drawing an oval with a crinkly edge and then blacking it in. It was accurate enough, but I realized that if I showed it to the waiter and he took it to the kitchen, he'd probably come back with an order of overdone meatballs. As matters stood he was still back there with the slip of paper containing the word *pruneau,* and it sounded as if he and his colleagues were engaged in a heated argument.

Then suddenly above the train noises came a mighty cry: "AHA! AH-PROOON-AH!"

It was repeated triumphantly by the others and in a moment our waiter came through the door, beaming, and he exclaimed, "Ah-prooon-ah!" and placed in front of my wife . . . a quart bottle of liquor.

We both started to laugh, and then to cry out, "No, no, no!" and "Non, non, non!" and the other passengers in the car now joined in the hilarity; apparently they had been watching our little drama all the while.

Now a Swiss air force officer arose from his table and came down the line and approached us.

"I speak small English," he said, bowing slightly. "You are a difficulty? Perhaps I can be of service."

"Prunes," I said. "Ma-*damn* wants prunes. You . . . know . . . what . . . is . . . prunes?" I showed him the little sketch and then said, "Fruit. Frooo-it. Froit. Froy. Dried le plum." He got it. He spoke in Italian to the waiter, and the waiter spoke in Italian to him, and then he said, "Very sorry. No prunes." I asked him if Switzerland is devoid of prunes. "It is known in this country," he said, "but only for people who is sick."

"Okay," I said. "It is not important. Please tell him bacon and werfs."

And so after a while we came to Lugano and we were following our baggage down the station platform when we happened to notice three white-capped heads sticking out of one of the train windows. The heads belonged to the kitchen crew. They were smiling at us, and waving river-dirtchy, and crying out, "Ah-proon! Prooon-ah! Ah-prooon-ah!" Somehow we felt good about the whole thing.

Later that same day we were in a speedboat traveling across Lake Lugano, the two of us occupying the seat which former King Farouk of Egypt had occupied one week earlier. The owner of the speedboat made much of this circumstance, displaying a fine sense of humor. He told us that he ought to charge us extra for sitting on the same seat that King Farouk had sat on; but he said he wouldn't charge us extra because the two of us fitted into the same space.

To my mind the adventure of the prunes far outshines the adventure of Farouk's seat. I don't contend that learning a foreign language is a bad thing to do. Obviously you'd be better off in France if you spoke French fluently. But I do say that if you're going traveling among foreigners, and you haven't found time to learn their language, go as you are . . . and order prunes.

22. THE STATE OF AMERICAN LETTERS

ONE DAY I sat down to write a letter to a man who had sicked his ferocious beagle on my gentle and home-loving cocker spaniel with obvious intent to mangle. This man, Poultney by name, is a neighbor of mine and by way of remonstrance I first tried the well-mannered personal approach. His response was to call me a series of harsh names and to conclude with: "Get off my property, you pigeon-toed popinjay."

I decided I didn't care much for this man and so, as I say, I sat down to write an indignant letter to him. I began in this fashion: "Dear Mr. Poultney:"

I sat and looked at that salutation for a while and then ripped the sheet of paper from my typewriter. It would never do. It wasn't adequate. I had come up against an old harassment — the problem of trying to cope with the inflexible deficiencies of our letter-writing etiquette.

We have sundered the atom and put it to work; we have developed automobiles that get out and wash off their own windshields; we have invented an electronic brain that composes songs and understands the writings of John Dewey; we have devised a machine that converts butter back into the cream that it originally was; we have discovered tranquilizing drugs that will render the E-string of a violin as limp as a wet noodle. Yet our letter-writing techniques have not been changed appreciably since the days when people used sand instead of blotters.

The problem is particularly vexatious in my case because, unlike most men who work at desks, I serve as my own secretary-typist. I correspond with large numbers of men and women who are not known to me in the flesh and I am required, by the archaic rules of epistolary intercourse, to address these people as if I were getting ready to marry them or as if they had recently rescued me from a burning building. I must use terms of deep friendship and endearment toward people who, for all I know, may be felons of the vilest stripe. I cannot understand why I should address that dog-killer Poultney as either "dear" or "mister" or even "sir." To call him "dear" is to call him glorious, worthy, honorable, and highly esteemed. To call him "sir" or "mister" is to bestow a respectful title on him, a title formerly reserved for men of rank, social authority, and dignity. This Poultney is wholly unworthy, dishonorable, has the social authority of a thrip, and is as far removed from dignity as a red-rumped baboon. Anybody who calls me a pigeon-toed popinjay is not going to get a respectful response. My letter to him was to be a bitter denunciation and a warning. It would never do for me to call him "dear sir." So I put a fresh sheet of paper in the typewriter and started again, trying to think of suitable antonyms for "dear" and for "sir." I thought of "Repulsive peasant" and "Splay-footed oaf" and "Knock-kneed lardhead." None of these seemed quite the exact thing I was after so I settled for the simple, noncommittal, "Listen, you!"

At length, after telling him off in the text of the letter, I came to the complimentary close. Complimentary indeed! I had no compliments to convey to this wretch. I refused to employ the customary word "Yours" because I was not his and never would be his. I could say "Sincerely" because my sentiments against him were genuinely sincere. I could not say "As ever" because that would indicate that my feelings toward him were the same as always; there had been a time when, little suspecting the evil that lurked in his heart, I had been quite friendly with him.

Then I remembered a letter written by the nine-year-old daughter of a friend who lives in New Jersey. This little girl, named Penelope, was infuriated by something she read in a New York newspaper column. She gave long and careful thought to the composition of a devastating retort to the columist. Her letter, as posted, read as follows:

Undear sir:
   What you said about Milton Berl applys to you
except you are jealous of Milton Berls success. Dont
you wish you were he instead of how you are sneaky.
                       Worst regards,
                       Penelope R———

134

I thought Penelope's salutation was a trifle more inspired then her uncomplimentary close but I borrowed the latter, nonetheless, and bade adieu to Poultney with "Worst regards."

Penelope had the right idea. Children, in fact, often take matters into their own hands and devise sensible techniques in their letter writing. I remember one summer when a neighbor boy went away to camp. He got sore at his parents because he felt they were not sending him enough pocket money. He began leaving off the salutation in his letters home; he'd be durned if he was going to salute such cruel and heartless and stingy people as "Dear Mom and Dad," or "Dearest Folks," or any similar guff. Apparently his juvenile mind recognized the new method as a great improvement over the old because all his letters after that, even when he went away to college, were minus salutations and minus complimentary closes. He is now grown to manhood and works as a junior executive in a New York City firm and I know that he flinches every time he has to preface his business letters with proper salutations and conclude them with dignified farewells. I know because I get occasional letters from him in which his resentment is clearly apparent. He concludes with such phrases as "Down with ink!" and "With malice toward all" and "There's a horse's patoot for every light on Broadway." Sometimes I suspect he has grown cynical.

There are other problems concerned with salutations which plague me from time to time. One such occurs in letters addressed to business houses in which I am required to salute the firm with "Gentlemen" or "Dear Sirs." I am required to do this even though I know that the company I am writing to is 85 or 90 per cent female. It disturbs my sense of balance to employ the salutation "Gentlemen" when I'm almost positive that my letter will be opened and acted upon by a woman. Marie L. Carney, in her book *Etiquette in Business,* lays down definite regulations in this area. She says that every business organization should be addressed as "Gentlemen" except in a case

135

where two women operate a firm *as a partnership*. They should be saluted with either "Ladies" or "Mesdames." I would go along with "Ladies" even though the females I'm addressing might not qualify, but I would never address anybody as "Mesdames," which is not pronounced "mesdames" but "meh-dom." I would never employ the term in a letter for the same reason that I would never enter a roomful of women and say, "Good evening, meh-dom" (unless, of course, I was cutting a caper). The thing that is a little confusing about Miss Carney's rules is her suggestion that if two women are in business together, not as a *partnership* but as a *company,* then they should be addressed as "Gentlemen." We have here a situation which could very well lead to the following:

Marie & Maude, Inc.,
Fifth Avenue,
New York, N. Y.

Gentlemen:

If you daffy females don't send me that panty girdle I ordered for my wife three weeks ago, I'll come down there and yank out all your hair.

> Forever thine,
> Hervey Gregg

This entire "Gentlemen" problem is so bewildering to the conscientious letter writer that I sometimes feel a Congressional committee should explore it and try to reform it. I'm not sure what could be done to straighten it out, but rather than employ an utterly foolish salutation, I'd prefer to address such firms with "Dear people" or "Howdy folks" or "You-all." Perhaps an entirely new word could be coined as meaning a mingling of the sexes in business. The word "gynecandrical," as in "gynecandrical dancing," derives from the Greek and means "men and women together." I've tried to convert it into a noun,

136

but "Dear Gynecand" and "Esteemed Gynecandric" somehow don't have the right flow. The new word to designate a person who is either male or female, or both, should be simpler, something like "Dear smalps" or "Dear furdick." I'll leave it up to Congress.

A business letter written by a lawyer in India has convinced me that we, the nation of commerce, have never really learned how to collect overdue accounts. Save for the inconsistency of his salutation, the Indian produced a dunning letter that is only a yard and a half short of magnificent. This is how it read:

Dear sir: Unless you pay the sum you owe me within seven days of this date, we shall take such steps as will cause you the utmost damned astonishment.

On occasion I get letters from individuals, strangers to me, whose signatures fail to reveal their sex. So many women nowadays have given names that might belong to men, names such as Leslie, Pat, Marion, Tony, Kim, Billy, Jo, Frankie, Jackie and so on. Quite often it's a case of "my folks wanted a boy." Just this moment a letter comes from Clyde Smith of North Carolina and it turns out to be *Miss* Clyde Smith. And I remember the long correspondence the late James Street had with *Who's Who in America* concerning his mother's name. Her name was William Street. Her son would write "William Street" under "mother's name" and *Who's Who* would write to him calling his attention to the error, and sending a new form. Mr. Street would fill it out just as before and return it, without explanation, and back it would come again. The hassle went on for six months before Mr. Street finally grew weary of it and told the *Who's Who* people that his mother's true name was William and for land's sake to leave him alone.

When I get a letter signed "Leslie Crumpleback" I assume it to be from a man, but there may be something in the text which hints that the writer is female. This usually puts me in such a pique that when I answer the letter, if I do at all, I employ the salutation:

Dear Mr. (Miss?) (Master?) (Mrs.?) Crumpleback:

I do this in spite of the directive from Miss Carney that if you don't know whether a woman is married or not, you should always address her as "Miss." I presume she means, also, that the same rule applies if you don't know whether a woman is a man or not. I simply don't like to operate that way.

It is my contention that we can get this whole problem of salutations and complimentary closes squared around without too much difficulty. We have actually made quite a bit of progress in the last hundred years. In eighteenth-century America a wife, when writing to her husband, almost invariably addressed him as "Dear sir." George Washington, in his letters to his mother, saluted her not as "Dear Mom" but as "Honoured Madam." In the time of Andrew Jackson it was fashionable for a man to employ such a vainglorious complimentary close as "I have the honor to be, Joe Smith." And during the same era even a challenge to a duel ended with "Yr Humbl & Obdt Svt, Sir."

That last sentiment would be appropriate if the letter were written by the footman or the butler or the upstairs maid. But to tack it on the end of an angry letter, as so many people did, is to carry tradition and custom much too far. The Duke of Wellington is the only man in history who, to my knowledge, ever handled that complimentary close properly. He sent an angry letter to one of his officers, concluding with: "I have the honor to be, sir, your humble and obedient servant (which you know damn well I am not), Wellington."

We got over all that sort of thing. I suspect that the whole business of the complimentary close is looked upon, by men of wit and intelligence, as pure fatuity. My suspicion is grounded on episodes I've seen in several English movies. In each case the Prime Minister or the Powerful Tycoon summons his secretary, dictates an important letter, and concludes with: "Yours and so forth and so forth and so forth get that off immejiately."

We've reformed, but not enough. I hope we can institute further sensible changes. If we don't, I have an idea I'll find myself employing such salutations as:

> Dear (to your own family) madam:

Or:

> Honorable (when you're asleep) sir:

---

23. NIX ON NIXIES

THE LOWEST FORM of humor, ranking 96.3 degrees beneath the pun, is the envelope half-witticism. The envelope humorist is the biological sport who splatters his feeble japery and sometimes his sarcasms on the face of the envelope which he sends through the mails. Right at the beginning I propose that his act be made a penitentiary offense.

The disease can be mild as in the case of the person who, rather than address his letter to plain "Mr. John Williams," does it this way:

Rt. Hon. J. Pilkington Williams, Esq., D.D.T., P.D.Q.

139

Or it achieves its more virulent form among those individuals who employ the rebus — drawing pictures and inventing complex conundrums on envelopes. A simple example:

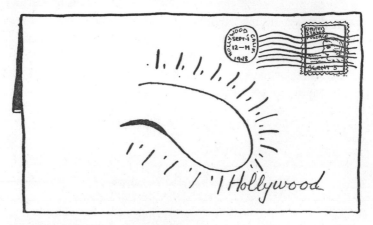

In time that letter probably would be delivered to Jimmy Durante. However, the real daring practitioner of this art form would not even include the place name "Hollywood." Just the nose and nothing else. He would then be taking a chance, I think, on having his letter delivered to the stockyards in Chicago and handed to a man celebrated locally for his skill in the dressing of beef tongues.

Every famous person whose name is associated with some physical characteristic or object which can be sketched on an envelope receives this type of mail: a park bench for Bernard Baruch, a shoe sole with a hole in it for Adlai Stevenson, et unhappily cetera. The late Fiorello H. La Guardia regularly received letters carrying no address other than a drawing of a big black hat. In a lesser degree my own identity is sometimes associated with a book title, *Low Man on a Totem Pole*. Once when I was employed at a movie studio in Hollywood a letter was delivered to me with nothing by way of address save a

140

drawing of a totem pole, with the bottom figure exaggerated. The letter had been a couple of months in transit and looked as if herds of unwashed elephants had walked upon it, but it finally found me. It had been devised by a male relative of mine with a screeching sense of humor. I have not spoken to him since the day I got it.

The post-office people have long had a name for the type of letter in which the address is given in a rebus, a conundrum, anagram, logogriph, or cryptogram. Such letters are known, and not affectionately, as *nixies*. In mythology a nixie is a water sprite. And what is a sprite? A sprite, says Webster, is a green woodpecker. Not a pecker of green wood, but a woodpecker with green plumage. Hence, by a curious twist of etymology, a person who invents and mails nixies could be called a green woodpecker. And should.

The woodpecker *verde* is no longer able to employ horn-rimmed glasses (once almost solely associated with Harold Lloyd) for the reason that several star television performers wear them nowadays, and whereas, in the past, a drawing of a bulging sweater would likely have meant Lana Turner, today Hollywood is teeming with girls who bulge sweaters. The dedicated green woodpecker, however, usually seeks higher planes on which to practice his hobby. He may start out by addressing his letters simply to "Bing" or "Pelvis" or "Lolly," but in time he goes on to greater glories. He comes up, perhaps, with a drawing of a bumblebee buzzing over a fiddle. Jack Benny, to be sure. Now he draws a picture of a common soldier walking with a general in his arms and if you look closely you discover that the general is Ulysses S. Grant. Cary Grant. Over the years the Hollywood post office has had to contend with a steady flow of nixies and the hard-harassed clerks there have developed a certain ingenuity in the business of deciphering them. Take this one, for example:

Its destination was recognized instantly: Ethyl Bury More.

Envelope humor is practiced widely among school kids, which is proof sufficient that the old-fashioned woodshed whaling ought to be revived, but don't think it's confined to the young. Men and women who otherwise show signs of possessing average intelligence often resort to it in the deluded belief that they are being clever. They even fancy that the post-office clerks and the letter carriers show their inventions around amidst paroxysms of laughter. How wrong they are! The post-office clerks would dearly love to belt them supine (or prone, depending on the direction in which they fall).

The efficiency of the modern automobile engine is such that the ordinary man, contemplating an eight-cylinder motor in the act of singing its lovely song, is inclined to regard the operation as a miracle. If he knows only the basic laws of that performance, he knows that the timing mechanism provides the miracle — the device that compels each of those eight cylinders to fire in its proper order at a speed that is dizzying to think about, and to go on doing it for months and even years without making an error involving so much as a small slice off a split second.

The same man, if he gave a moment's thought to it, would

realize that the post-office department is geared in much the same way, and that the chief element in its efficiency is timing. It is still to me something of a minor miracle that I can slap a seven-cent stamp on a letter, deposit it in an iron box on a street corner in New York, and feel certain that it will be dropped on the desk of my friend in Los Angeles the following day. If it fails to reach its destination on the following day, the blame may well lie with the nixie artists. Their playfulness has the same effect on the efficiency of the post office that a pot of bean soup would have if it were poured into the fuel tank of that eight-cylinder engine.

It's bad enough that post-office workers have to contend with the cave-writing of the nation's illiterates and semiliterates, and the stupidities of people who are simply fuzzy-headed and careless. The New York City post office, which handles 10 per cent of the nation's business, receives nearly 200,000 pieces of misdirected mail every day. Each working day about 60,000 pieces of mail come in without street addresses, and 660 parcels with no addresses whatever on them — the senders have simply wrapped them and tied them up and thrown them in the mailbox.

Illiteracy is a sort of disease and shouldn't be penalized, but there ought to be a law forbidding the use of the mails to people whose handwriting looks like an eggbeater struck by lightning. (Last phrase by courtesy of Mark Twain).

A clearly addressed, succinct and to-the-point envelope is a thing of sheer beauty to a postal employee in view of the vast amount of undecipherable mail he has to handle. One New York postal clerk tabulated 197 different spellings of "Chicago" that came to hand in a few months. Among the more bizarre were: Zizabo, JagJago, Jaiijo, Hipaho, Hizago, Sheshego, and Chaque-chico.

In Los Angeles a man named Chris Mulrain turned out a

pamphlet a few years ago, pleading with the public to exercise more care in addressing mail. He told of one letter addressed to:

> Mr. Taylor,
> The Man Who Lifts 150 Pounds With His Ears,
> Pomona, Calif.

And another:

> Gift Shop,
> Next Door South of Loan Co.

Mr. Mulrain's pamphlet reminded Mike Jackson, the Los Angeles columnist, that he once received a letter addressed to "Mike J., Can Hold His Breath 74 Seconds, California." And in the New York City post office not long ago a clerk came upon this:

> The Station To Which You Are Listening,
> New York, N.Y.

I once discussed this whole problem with Albert Goldman, who spent eighteen years as New York City's postmaster. Mr. Goldman is a man with a sentimental eye, holding the belief that the main function of the post-office system is the dissemination of loving thoughts and gladful tidings. He is, moreover, a man with a strong element of humor in his make-up. Yet he has never been either sympathetic or amused at the prospect of people who deliberately pour bean soup into the miraculous machine, thus impairing its proud efficiency.

"The separators and distributors who work in the post offices of the nation," Mr. Goldman said, "are geared to a certain efficiency which they have developed through years of training and scheme study. Most of these workers take great pride in the number of pieces of mail they can handle in a given period; it is the same sort of pride that a golfer takes in a consistently good

144

score. It is not likely then that these people are amused by the nixie nuisance."

Out of his years as postmaster Mr. Goldman recalled all manner of tricks employed by the dumb alecks, the pourers of bean soup, the green woodpeckers. Occasionally a letter comes in with name of the city in Morse code, as: –·–· ·–·· · ···– · ·–·· ·– –· –·· for Cleveland. Others employ musical notation in working out an address. Or cryptograms of varying complexity, the simplest being the 2-18-15-15-11-12-25-14 as meaning Brooklyn. Then there are the nixie chemists who address letters to "H_2O bury" and "H_2O town" for Waterbury and Watertown. One of the most famous nixie devices was this:

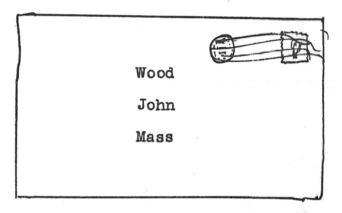

Wood

John

Mass

The letter addressed in that seemingly mysterious fashion was meant for John Underwood, Andover, Mass. It is the nearest thing to cleverness I have ever encountered in the work of the nixie people. Yet it doesn't double me up.

During the preparation of this book I've kept an eye on my own mail. It has included two letters from an anonymous correspondent who addresses me in care of Emily Brontë, Wuthering Heights. I did not laugh. Another letter carried the identifying phrase, "Lousiest Author on Earth." I was not amused.

145

Still another came for "H. Allen Smith, Dean of American Nothing." I didn't even smile. The exterior of an envelope is not the proper place for a correspondent to demonstrate either his sarcasm or his comicality. There's plenty of room inside for such insipidities. The post-office employees don't think he's funny and would enjoy watching him simmer gently in oil. And the people on the receiving end of his green woodpeckering consider him not a humorist but a fool. He will, therefore, be doing everyone a large favor, including himself, if he will cease his operations or, barring that, book passage on the first *ill-fated* rocket ship leaving for the moon.

24. THE HAZARDS OF STORYTELLING

AMONG the sovereign liberties implicit in the constitution is the right of every man to tell a funny story. No matter how unfunny it may turn out, he still is permitted by law to tell a joke and not be put in jail for it. (Now you can see what a really great country this is.) And even if he flubs it and fluffs it and fouls it up in the end, he still need have no fear of the firing squad. All he needs fear is me.

For vague and illogical reasons a writer of humor is subjected during all his professional life to an almost continuous bombardment of funny stories, and these are told to him by two classes of people: (1) those who are proficient in the art of storytelling and (2) those who shouldn't be allowed out. The second class, I sometimes think, outnumbers the first by eighteen hundred to one.

146

I am a semipro writer of humor and live under an incessant rain of jokes, yet sometimes I make an effort to be tolerant even toward the clumsiest of the narrators. For one thing, I often find amusement in the spectacle of a blundering and graceless storyteller, for his struggles with a joke can be much funnier than the joke itself.

Ring Lardner wouldn't listen to a joke. Whenever a person came up to him and said, "Have you heard the one about . . ." Lardner would snap, "I heard it," and walk away. Once someone asked him why he did this and he said, "Because people are such rotten storytellers."

Frank Sullivan believes that raconteurs ought to be put through tests and then licensed like surgeons and notaries and dogs, and that any unlicensed person caught in the act of trying to bootleg a funny story should be assigned to homesteading at Alcatraz.

All this is a rather violent and negative approach to a problem that needs serious attention. For one thing, it requires great patience and fortitude to indulge in joke-telling nowadays. Our system of etiquette has not kept pace with the swiftness of our communications. If a screechingly funny story pops up in, say, the Battery neighborhood of Charleston, it will have spread to every remote cranny of the country within three and three-quarters minutes. By the time it gets to me, everybody else on earth has heard it. Most people are still polite and when I try to tell it, they will say they haven't heard it, but I can always tell that they really *have* heard it and are just being kind; still I must go on with it and at the end they go into a fit of neighing, or indulge in the unattractive kind of laughter known by the unattractive name of cachinnation. Such people are among the meanest human beings on earth. There is only one class that is meaner — those who wait until you're through with your story and then say, "Yeh, I heard it, only the way I heard it, it went like this . . ." and then proceed to tell *their* version of the story, in which the only difference is that the fella's name is John, instead of Charlie, the way *he* heard it.

Too many people look upon humor as mere frivolity, and upon a funny story as a triviality, worth perhaps a vagrant smile or even a well-articulated titter and then to be cast aside and forgotten. This may be the reason why so many people are forever saying, "I hear hundreds of funny stories but somehow I never seem able to remember any of them." A joke, or funny story, in the hands of the right person, is an art form as surely as a sonnet or a symphony is an art form.

Bret Harte said that the funny story, the one that is told by word of mouth, was the father of the literary short story. Please note that the most skillful of our short-story writers are people who put an enormous amount of labor into achieving the exact effect they are after. James Thurber rewrites some of his stories as many as thirty times; Frank O'Connor, one of the really great masters of the short-story form, has revised a story fifty times before turning it loose. The same loving care should be given to the style and the method of telling a funny story.

Stephen Leacock felt that amateur storytellers should make an effort to discipline themselves — to the extent of *not* telling stories at all. "Few people," said Leacock, "realize how extremely difficult it is to tell a story so as to reproduce the real fun of it . . . It needs the right words, with every word in its proper place. Here and there, perhaps once in a hundred times, a story turns up which needs no telling . . . No narrator however clumsy can altogether fumble it." There is much wisdom in Mr. Leacock's declaration, except for that last part. I know a narrator who could and would fumble that unfumble-able story — an acquaintance of mine, or, rather, I know her real well . . . to be perfectly truthful about it, she's a relative of mine . . . oh, hell, it's my wife.

There are some people, it is true, who are congenitally unable to tell a funny story. It is one of the great mysteries of human nature why they persist at the business, for they suffer untold misery as they bumble and blunder along. "I heard a real good one the other day," they'll say. "I'm not sure I remember how it goes, but anyway, there was this dentist and he . . ." Of course they don't remember how it goes. Maybe they remember up to the punch line, at which point they begin chewing their fingers and grimacing and saying, "Oh, darn it all, now what *was* it he said after that? Well, I just can't remember it to save my life, but I want to tell you it was a scream, what he said, if I could only remember it, you'd laugh your head off."

Or their stubbornness takes another direction when they say, "I'm not any good at dialect, but I'll try it anyway — there was this Scotchman walking down a country road and . . ." It turns out to be horribly true — he's not any good at dialect. He is, in fact, so awful at dialect that his story often sounds like the gibble-gabble of a jungle medicine man. The temptation is strong to throttle him where he stands, but I manage to put it down by thinking of a man I know who amalgamates dialects when he tells a story, saying something like this: "Well, so Pat says to Mike, 'Bejabbers, me bye, und vy dun't you esking hah-cum all dem dere li'l chirren am sho nuff eading veenervurst mit zower-graut befo dey go to da moom pitch in-a da beeg ceety?' "

Robert Benchley once undertook the assignment of instructing people in the art of telling funny stories. The joke, he said firmly, must be in a language we can understand, it must be spoken loudly enough for us to hear it, and it must begin with the letter W.

Actually there are some sensible guideposts for the person who is unhandy at telling stories. He goes blundering along his unmerry way simply because nobody ever bothers to tell him that there's a right way and a wrong way.

Don't oversell your story at the beginning. Don't tell people,

"This one will kill ya," or "This is the funniest story you ever heard in your life." And don't preface your story with bursts of anticipatory laughter. The funniest stories are those in which the narrator acts as if he had no idea in the world there is anything at all comical about what he's saying.

Be prepared for interruptions, especially if you are in a group. The world is full of point-killers, beginning with the hostess who breaks into the best part of your story with, "Oh, come on and have some more peas." or "Why, Myra, I hadn't even noticed that you've had your hair dyed." A point-killer needn't even be human. I once had an oak tree ruin a story for me. I was in the home of friends in North Carolina, telling a marvelous story about a hired hand and a mule. Suddenly there was a crash as if the Day of Judgment were at hand — a huge limb from an oak tree had come unhooked in the wind and crashed through the roof of the sun porch, wrecking that end of the house. I never did get to finish my story.

The best American storytellers, incidentally, are the Southerners. They collect and retain good stories, remembering how the words and the sentences fit together, and they don't hurry themselves when they tell them. The rest of us can learn from them. Take it easy. Go slow. Drawl.

If you are a good storyteller you already know it and the rules don't apply. There are important exceptions, anyway, to all of the rules. You might be warned that you should beware of digressions, of getting away from the main point, of veering off on a tangent. Yet the funniest story of all the funny stories told by the great Mark Twain was the one about "Grandfather's Old Ram," which consists altogether of digressions and tangents.

The rule says you shouldn't laugh before or during or after telling a joke. Yet Fred Allen did it consistently, laughing and chuckling at his own stories, and Sam Levinson laughs more at his own jokes than anybody in his audience.

150

In most cases of clumsy and ineffective storytelling, the fault is one of carelessness. The best of all storytellers are actors. They know how to handle dramatic effects and they know timing. But more important, they know the great value of rehearsal — of knowing their lines.

An expert raconteur will tell you that there is more fun to be gained in telling a good story, and telling it effectively, than there is in listening to a good story. And he will tell you that the most important single element of his art is memorizing. If you have a story which you like and want to tell to other people, get it well organized in your head, rehearse it until you feel certain that there's no chance of your forgetting any part of it. If it's worth telling at all, it's worth memorizing.

Having committed your story to memory, the next step is to set up a procedure to be followed just in case you *do* fumble the telling. All great storytellers have "fluff lines" which they can use to great effect if they fumble. At one of the Emmy awards dinners Milton Berle was the hit of the show because of a twelve-minute monologue. And the biggest yock in his act was a "fluff line." He stumbled over a long word, mispronouncing it, grinned sheepishly, and then said, as if speaking to himself, "Had my nose fixed, now my mouth don't work."

25. THE SHABBY FRIAR JOKE

ALMOST EVERYONE knows what a shaggy dog story is. This offbeat type of joke had a wide popularity a few years back and is said to have originated in London. The story goes that an English gentleman put an ad in the papers offering a reward for the return of a lost dog — a big shaggy dog. A day or two later a man appeared at his door with a big shaggy dog on the end of a rope.

"Did you advertise for the return of a big shaggy dog?" the man on the doorstep asked. The gentleman glanced down at the animal and then responded, with a touch of acerbity, "Yes, but not *that* shaggy."

There is another type of witticism that seems to be achieving wide currency today. Through the authority vested in me by nobody I have named it the Shabby Friar Joke. It is a sort of an upside-down antecedency quip, or a reverse sequitur with backlash. It is by no means a new humoristic device, as I intend to show.

Mr. Clifton Fadiman has lately announced himself as a devotee of a certain eighteenth-century German professor named G. C. Lichtenberg. One of Professor Lichtenberg's observations which tickles the fancy of Mr. Fadiman is this: it is astonishing that a cat has two holes placed in its skin at precisely the correct positions for the eyes to see through.

What Professor Lichtenberg is dealing with here is an excellent example of the Shabby Friar Joke. It is a linguistic contrivance that has fascinated me since that day in London when I first read about the Carmelite friar. Three or four hundred years ago this friar, clad in a shabby tunic, stood on the banks of the Thames and marveled at the surpassing wisdom of God in arranging for navigable rivers to flow past the larger towns.

There has been a continuing awareness of the Shabby Friar Joke in my family in recent years for the peculiar reason that we are in love with Mexico. In the jungles of Yucatán there is a beautiful hotel called the Mayaland. It stands at the edge of the Mayan ruins of Chichen Itza, and guests who sit on the long ground-floor terrace can look across the lobby and see, framed in the exact center of the arched hotel entrance, the crumbling

152

structure known as the Observatory, which was erected some time in the ninth century.

One afternoon my wife and I were sitting on the Mayaland terrace and she was gazing at this picture-postcard vista. Finally she spoke.

"Wasn't it thoughtful of the ancient Mayas," she said, "to build the ruins of the Observatory so they could always be seen through the doorway of this hotel?"

I suspect she had been thinking of our Mexican friend Carlos Campo, who escorts us around his native tierra from time to time and who frequently employs this type of witticism without ever having heard of Mr. Fadiman's German professor or my own Carmelite friar. Just a few weeks earlier Carlos had taken us up to the ruins of Monte Alban, which surmount a lofty peak rising abruptly above the city of Oaxaca in southern Mexico. As we reached the crest of the mountain where the ruins stand, I looked back at the town far below us, and Carlos said, "Please notice, amigo, how ess-smart was the Zapotecs to build their sacred city right here where they would always have a nice view of the whole city of Oaxaca."

Another time I was in a Veracruz drugstore with Carlos. He was trying on sunglasses. Suddenly he turned to me and said, "Look how ess-smart was God to put the ears in the exact right place to hold on the eyglasses." I'm quite certain that Carlos never heard of a remark by Voltaire — that the human nose was designed especially to support eyeglasses.

The basic element, or the elemental basis, of the Shabby Frair Joke is the *non sequitur*. In it cause usually stems from effect. Personally I would be content to call a *non sequitur* by its simple Latin name, but Webster defines it this way: "Any fallacy resulting from a simple conversion of a universal affirmative proposition or from the transposition of a condition and its consequent; — called also *fallacia consequentis.*" I may know

153

what that means, but if I do, I'm sure I don't. Still, and notwithstanding this garble of words, I have undertaken a diligent search of my files, my memory, my books, and I have picked the brains of my friends, seeking quips or expressions that qualify, or almost qualify, in the category of the Shabby Friar Joke. I have come up with a dispatch case full of them, a few of which follow:

It has been seriously argued [says Bertrand Russell] that rabbits have white tails so that it will be easier for men to shoot them.

A lovesick student at Fordham University wandered into a laboratory, stumbled over a Bunsen burner and lurched against the university's seismograph, setting off a calamitous earthquake in Guatemala.

On a hot summer day in a town in Arkansas, the owner of a barbershop made an important scientific decision. He took down the screen door at the front entrance to his shop. People asked him why. "I finely figgered out," he said, "that a screen door jest natcheral attracks flies."

From the works of Artemus Ward: "I met a man in Oregon who hadn't any teeth — not a tooth in his head — yet that man could play on the bass drum better than any man I ever met."

Herman Hickman used to tell a story about a party of hunters arriving at a country store in the remote hills of Tennessee. The hunters were worried about the weather, and the hillbilly storekeeper told them he had just heard over the radio that it was going to rain. So the hunters decided they should turn back. "Oh, no," protested the hillbilly. "The man said it's gonna rain but I wouldn't be a-puttin' too much stock in it — it's only a little old cheap radio."

Neill Beck of Malibu was asked once about the quality of property in a certain beach area north of where she lives. "I wouldn't buy up there," she advised, "because in my opinion the ocean is too close to the shore."

154

A French philosopher once remarked: "How stupid for all the magnificent volcanoes to be placed on the tops of the ugliest mountains."

There is a story in the original Joe Miller joke book, published in 1739, which tells of a melting sermon being preached in a country churchyard. All present fell to weeping except one man who, being asked why he did not shed tears with the others, said, "Oh, I couldn't. I belong to another parish."

I once heard a man say he was from Tennessee, and another man remarked, "Oh, yes, that's the state shaped like an auto license plate."

In the same category as the Fordham seismograph joke is one about a man who brought home a thermometer to fasten outside his kitchen door. His wife, who had asked him to fetch a jar of artichoke hearts, mistook the flattish package containing the thermometer for the artichoke hearts, and put it in the refrigerator. Up to that time it had been a steaming hot July day, but now the temperature began dropping out of the 80's, plummeting swiftly to the middle 40's, with the consequence that everybody caught cold.

Somewhere I have read the statement that "the only time Shakespeare was ever any good was when he wrote things to be quoted."

And in Maine someone asked a character named Leete True if he believed in infant baptism. "God yes," he responded, "I've seen it done."

Just recently I've learned that Abraham Lincoln once committed a fine Shabby Friar Joke. He said he thought it a most wondrous thing that man was so designed that his legs were always long enough to reach the ground. Abe's observation has brought to mind that I am the inventor of at least a couple of qualifiers. I used them in a book, quite a few years back, before *I* had ever heard of the Carmelite friar. I once wrote that the little flap of gristle known as the tragus, which stands in front of the opening of the human ear, was put there by a kindly Mother Nature for the benefit of artillerymen, who press their fingers against it when firing their big guns to avoid rupturing their eardrum.

And reflecting on *that,* I found myself standing before a mirror, glowing with wonderment at the cleverness involved in the construction of the human head and neck — clearly designed by Nature to accommodate the hangman's noose. At least *my* head and neck look that way.

26. MOMENT OF TRUTH— IRISH STYLE

THAT richly expressive adjective "Irish" goes well with daises and diamonds, sweepstakes and stews, setters and terriers, potatoes and peanuts, linen and whisky, and now James E. Palmer of Indianapolis reminds me that there is a type of syntactical blunder known as the Irish bull.

In previous chapters I have considered the spoonerism and the malapropism. The Irish bull is utterly unlike either of these two; it depends more on logical inconsistencies than on the twisting of words, and it is a close relative of the Shabby Friar Joke. The *Oxford English Dictionary* defines the Irish bull as "a self-contradictory proposition; in modern use, an expression containing a manifest contradiction in terms or involving a ludicrous inconsistency unperceived by the speaker." Sometimes it is almost comical, the highfalutin language a big full-grown dictionary will use to explain a simple proposition. So, just in case it still isn't clear, we have a couple of quick examples.

The aforementioned Mr. Farmer, a newspaperman and

publicist, tells us that in Indianapolis there is a collector of Irish humor named H. A. O. Speers, and from his archives come the following bulls: The chairman of an Irish corporation said to a critic, "Perhaps you think that in our board half do the work and half do nothing. As a matter of fact, the reverse is the case." The other Speers example: An Irish legislator said in a speech, "What is likely to happen? In my opinion nothing is likely to happen. That is what always happens in England."

No matter how stubborn their claim, the Irish cannot hold exclusive ownership of bulls. It is said in the books that the Irish bull got its name from one Obadiah Bull, an Irish lawyer of the eighteenth century, who was famous for his blundering speech. Other authorities deny this assertion with heat, saying that Chaucer used the word "bole" as meaning a verbal mistake a century before Obadiah Bull's time. Personally I see no merit whatever in the Chaucer argument. That Chaucer was the worst speller that ever came down the pike, and God alone knows what he might have meant when he put down the word "bole." He is not to be trusted.

A man named Edgeworth once wrote an essay titled "Irish Bulls," in which it was his aim to prove that bulls are not Irish. It is my understanding that this Edgeworth was so persuasive in his argument that he proved there is no such thing as a bull. Edgeworth reminds me, somehow, of Godfrey Turner, who grew famous in London as the author of an essay titled "The Inns of Jamaica," the first line of which was, "There are no inns in Jamaica."

The only triple, or three-legged, bull we have encountered is not Irish at all, but came from the lips of a South American who, at a dinner party in New York, remarked that he had a charming wife but unfortunately no children. "You see," he explained, "my wife is unbearable." The company could not suppress its astonishment and he realized he had blundered, so he said, "I mean, my wife is inconceivable." And realizing that his

157

second try was also wrong, he finished up by almost shouting. "What I mean to say is, she is impregnable."

The most celebrated Irish bull roarer was Sir Boyle Roche, a member of Parliament. Among his classical remarks were these:

"Why should we beggar ourselves for posterity? What has posterity ever done for *us?*"

"Half the lies those Tories tell about us are not true."

"All along the untrodden paths of the future he could see the footprints of an unseen hand." (This is first cousin to the remark attributed to Samuel Goldwyn. "I want to go someplace where the hand of man has never set foot.")

"The country is overrun with absentee landlords."

"A man could never be in two places at the same time . . . unless, of course, he was a bird."

I am prepared to show that we in the United States have all but taken over the bull, that we excel in its use somewhat more than other peoples. First, however, let us have a look at some additional Irish bulls which I've been able to find in various books of humor and folklore:

Father, to a whining child: "What a nuisance! The next time I take you any place I'll leave you home!"

"An Irishman is never completely at peace except when he's fighting."

"I'd die first before I'd be buried in an English cemetery."

A candidate for office in Ireland, angling for the working-man's vote, said in a speech, "I was born without a penny in my pocket."

An Irish *Handbook for Cyclists* recommended: "The best way to pass a cow on the road is to keep behind him."

A lady invalid, returning from the seashore, told a friend, "It has done me a world of good. I feel like another woman. In fact I am myself again."

An Irish servant girl in New York wrote home to say that

her employers were so rich that their flannel petticoats were all made of silk.

A Dublin shop advertised that it had "a small quantity of sherry in stock that was drunk by Queen Victoria."

An Irishman awoke in the night, saw a ghost in the room, seized his shotgun and let go a blast. He then discovered that the ghost had been his shirt hanging on the bedpost. "Thank God," he said, "that I wasn't in it when I fired!"

An Irish architect said solemnly: "Where will you find any modern building that has lasted as long as the old ones?"

An Irishman said to a young priest: "I hope I live to hear you preach my funeral sermon." And an Irishman said to another Irishman, "May you live to eat the chicken that scratches over your grave."

The English people have always been great hands with the bull. Disraeli was famous for a whole series of blunders. Once in Parliament he declaimed: "It is curious to observe the various substitutes for paper before its invention." The Eighth Duke of Devonshire was overheard to remark, "Last night I dreamed that I was addressing the House of Lords. Then I woke up, and by God I was!" An English shopkeeper, asked about the durability of a piece of goods, said, "Madam, it will wear forever and make you a petticoat afterwards."

Both tribes are involved in the story of the Englishman engaged in writing a letter in a tavern. He wrote: "I would say more but there is a damned nosy Irishman looking over my shoulder and reading every word of this." Whereupon the Irishman cried out, "You lie, you scoundrel!"

Groucho Marx's "I'd horsewhip you if I had a horse" is a true example of a bull even though the "ludicrous inconsistency" was deliberate. Shakespeare committed quite a few, for example, "Caesar did never wrong save with just cause." So did Samuel Johnson, as in, "Every monumental inscription should be in Latin, for that being a dead language it will ever live." And so did the Bible, as in, "Then the angel of the Lord went forth and smote in the camp of the Assyrians a hundred and fourscore and five thousand; and when they arose early in the morning behold, they were all dead corpses."

The bulls of newspaper copyreaders — the men who compose the headlines — are often delightful. Here are two examples: FATHER OF TWELVE SHOT; MISTAKEN FOR RABBIT, and EGG-LAYING CHAMPIONSHIP WON BY LOCAL WOMAN.

But now to get to some purely American bulls. I have gone through my own eccentric files and also my memory and dredged up the following:

In Illinois, Abe Lincoln was once riding his horse along a country road. The horse suddenly flung a hind foot forward and got it caught in the stirrup. Lincoln looked down, saw what had happened, and then said, "Well, horse, if you're gonna get on, *I'm* gonna get off."

A Hollywood producer said his wife "wanted to have her portrait painted here in Beverly Hills, but I'm sending her to Europe to have it done by one of the old masters."

Mrs. Maurine Grau of Orlando, Florida, tells of the time she was in the kitchen making a fancy noodle dish. Her maid stood by, watching, and when the operation was finished, said, "Just to think, if I'd a died last night I'd never a knowed about this."

A preoccupied lady, leaving a party with her husband, said to the hostess, "It was so nice of us to come."

A young man of my acquaintance employed a word whose meaning obviously wasn't too clear to him, for it involves a gymnastical impossibility: "There she stood," he said, "With her behind akimbo."

A speaker at a banquet began his oration: "Now, before I start I want to say something."

The following sign was posted in a tavern: "The Management Reserves the Right to Exclude Any Lady They Think Proper."

A schoolteacher smiled at a man on a bus, then realized she didn't know him, and apologized: "Oh, excuse me. I mistook you for the father of two of my children."

A male instructor in a wartime school for WAVES asked his class, "What signal would you give if you were coming out of your slip stern first?"

A cleaning woman mailed a "Deepest Sympathy to You" card to her employer, after writing on it, "My mother dead. I no come work this week. Opal."

A famous joke which is also a bull involves a telephone call at 3 A.M., with the caller saying, "I hope I didn't disturb you." And the reply, "Oh, not at all. I had to get up and answer the phone anyway."

A classified ad: "Girl, 21, would like job operating elevator in office building. Has no experience so would like to start in low building."

Senator Joseph McCarthy, asked what he thought of a statement made by another senator, said, "It's the most unheard of thing I ever heard of."

A Broadway character named Solly Violinsky once refused to accept a much needed loan of a thousand dollars "because the party isn't reliable."

Jim Devers of the old New York *World* was telling a story one day when he said, "And through that door came the biggest man God ever made. The *biggest* man God ever made! And right behind him, as God is my judge, came one *three times as big!*"

James Farmer reports that some years ago in the Indiana Legislature a school truancy bill was under discussion. Representative William H. Herring of Linton warned the House: "This is one of the touchiest of issues we'll touch upon. Some

161

are not parents, but they have children who will be parents some day."

An itinerant preacher was once holding a revival in Texas and in the course of a sermon was describing Hell in eloquent and frightening terms. Finally a little man arose from his seat in the audience, raised his hand for quiet, and then objected: "There couldn't be no sitch of a place. Th' people wouldn't stand fer it!"

It was a Texas cattle baron, accused of land-grabbing, who took the witness stand and testified: "It's a lie. I don't want all the land in Texas — jist the part that jines onto my place."

Out of my own past I remember a political declaration I heard years ago in Florida. It has a bullish flavor and it points up the confusion some people get into when they try to deal with the pronoun *whom*. A backwoods politician was making a speech in the town of Sebring, and he said, "I want you folks to know that I have always tried to serve the common people, *of whom I am one of which.*"

27. WHAT IS MOGLATION?

IN THE EARLY 1930's there was circulated quite widely in the United States an essay purportedly written by a school child on the subject "The Horse." This is how it went:

The horse is a very noble quadrupped but when it is angry it will not do so. He is ridden on the spinal chord by the bridle and sadly the driver places his foots on the stirrups and drives his lower limbs across the saddle and drives his animal to the meadow. He has four legs. These are the weapons on which he runs. He also defends himself by extending these in the rear. They have got tails but not so long as the cow. She has no children and it was the same with her mother.

Though this small essay is considered to be a classic of its kind, I am suspicious of it. I sense the presence of an adult hand in some of its portions. On the other hand, I know that a second-grader in Charlotte, North Carolina, actually wrote this:

I cried at my aunts wedding. She cried too. Carol and Henry kissed. Her wedding dress is pretty. The Pucketts said marriage vowels. The wedding was very pretty. Her rings was pretty. She was pretty. He was pretty. The car said Watch Charlotte Grow.

And I know, too, that a fifth-grader in Asheville wrote what I consider to be one of the greatest poems in the language — a couplet that contains Truth if ever poetry contained Truth, as follows:

AUTUMN
The autumn days are here
You always expect them this time of year.

For the reason that in recent years I have produced two books containing collections of prose and poetry written by the very young, people all over the country are steadily sending me additional examples of juvenilia. The accumulation of material is rapidly approaching the point where I may have to lease the big Granville barn, down the hill, as a storehouse for it.

As I have declared previously, children are much better writers than their elders because no pressures affect them. They strike out boldly with no regard for the piddling laws that deal with slander and libel. Mark Twain once remarked that children are the most competent of all letter writers because "they tell all they know, and then stop." And Oliver Wendell Holmes said that "pretty much all the honest truth-telling there is in the world is done by children." Still, they are capable sometimes of being esoteric if not confusing. Mrs. Walter J. Caron of Salem, Massachusetts, has sent me a sort of word list compiled by her son when he was eight. This is the way it reads, in bold, penciled lettering:

> NO — TREPASSING ON THIS PROPERTY
> YOUR — SUITCASE — IS — IN — YOU
> R — CLOSET
> INDEPENDENCE
> LIBERTY
> TOURNIQUET
> EXTENCE
> UNBELIEVEBLE
> MOGLATION
> SURVEYLING

Mrs. Caron begs me to find a definition for the word "moglation." From time to time she has worried about "extence" as well as "surveyling," but she tells me that "moglation" has been driving her half-crazy for ten years. "It haunts me to this day," she says, and I understand perfectly, for it is beginning to haunt me, too.

Children are capable of bitterness in their writings, but they are also capable of great compassion. Here is a note which a ten-year-old boy left under his mother's pillow:

Dear Mum: I just wrote this short letter to thank you for all you have dun for me in the past. I thank you from the bottom of my heart. I just cant thank you for all you have dun for me so now I thank you agian from the very very very bottom of my heart
                                        from your loving son

Or, consider a note which the principal of a Michigan school found on the kitchen table when he arrived home one evening. The note was the work of his seven-year-old daughter. The heading consisted of a crude drawing of two grownups with tears streaming from their eyes, and the caption, DONT DO THIS. The typewritten text of the note read:

164

To Daddy from Karen. God bless you Daddy. I am writing this letter only to you but show it to mother. I am running away. But please dont feel bad. Fairwell to all the family. God bless all of you. I'm sorry that this is the way it goes. MERRY CHRISTMAS. I really dont want to do this but thats just the way it goes.

signed Karen.

Karen's father tells me that she had no intention whatever of running away — that the letter was simply an exercise of her imagination.

The scribbling kids are quite often guilty of superb unconscious humor. A music teacher in Jefferson City, Mo., cites these passages from essays written by his pupils:

Bach was the most famous composer in the world and so was Handel.

Haydn died in 1809 and is still dead.

Paganini was a famous fiddler. He fiddled with many of the greatest singers in Europe.

Personally I have no quarrel with grammatical eccentricity among the children, being somewhat eccentric in that direction myself. I have an essay written by a seventh-grader in my own suburban neighborhood on the subject "How to Behave on a School Bus." It is an essay in one sentence, and that sentence contains 328 words, which gives it a Faulknerish tone. This is how it goes:

DONOT FULL AROUND

When on the bus you must sit in a seat and not full around or jump over the seats, or fight or throw paper around because you will get the bus driver nervous and he might reck and kill all of the people on the bus, and never chew gum in the bus driver ear because he my get nervous and reck and kill all of the people in the bus, and never talk to the bus driver when he is driving because he might reck and you must not flash lights in the bus in back of you or in front of you because you my reck the bus and kill all the people in the bus, and you must not scream because you will make the bus driver reck and kill all the people in the bus and you must not show any kind of paper or paper claps in the bus because you my hurt some one or you my hit the bus driver and he my reck and kill all of the people on the bus, and never talk back to the bus driver or any one else, and donot every shot rubber bands on the bus because you my hurt the bus driver and he my reck and kill all of the people on the bus, and you must not ful around at the bus stop, and never tak anybody elses books and throw around that donot belong to you, and donot take any seat apart or step on them or kick them and donot rip them or write on them or mark them up in any way and never touch the gas pedal with your foot or touch any other pedal, and never open the door because you might fall out and kill your self and never take any screws out of the seats or any other part of the school bus or any bus.

It is my opinion that neither Faulkner nor Hemingway nor the late Thomas Wolfe could have said it more effectively.

Beverly Anne Holcombe of Grand Island, New York, has sent along a group of succinct essays she wrote on "Wild Life" when she was eight. One example is sufficient to demonstrate Beverly's stark economy of words:

PORCUPINE

The Porcupine lives in the woods and is full of needles it has a lot of enimys here are some of them the bear the lion the tiger and humans

My accumulation of juvenile writings covers almost every academic subject known to education. Even literary criticism. A boy in Alaska has written me a letter on ruled tablet paper saying:

My pairnts read your book and mom said A WOMAN COULED DO BETTER. I couled write a better book but a book is to long for me to write now because I half to pick cramberies but I will write a short story.

Skateing on our lake

We went skateing and mom fel into her waste by the beaver house. HELP IM DROUNDING she yeled. NOBODYS GOING TO DROUND QUIT YELING WILE I GET A STICK YOU

CAN GRAB THE OTHER END OF pop said. moms teeth ratled and she was shifering then pop said RUN AROUND FAST AND SWING YOUR ARMS. our dog is a wimerainer our labbedor that got stold was better.

A case that seems to involve an actual drounding is narrated by an eight-year-old girl whose letter was forwarded by an artist friend in California. It goes:

Dear Sybil I wanted to write to you sooner. But I have been busy. I can't come down I have no way. Do you remember Wiley? him his sister and Brother inlay went fishing Wiley got his hook caught dick went out and unhook it he went down in a hole Jackie went in after him got him by the hair and pulled him in Just as got him to the bank he said LET GO she Let go and he drowned well thats how it goes
Love Evelyn

Please note the special technique employed by Evelyn in her report of this exciting event. In the beginning, or the dull part, she uses punctuation, but when Wiley gets his hook caught and all the tumult and heroics begin to develop, everything runs together, punctuation is abandoned, and the prose takes on the feverish tenor of the chase in a western movie.

A prominent writer of my acquaintance has shown me a note he received from a schoolgirl, who was quite obviously trying to impress him with her intelligence. The note concluded:

Right now I am in the mist of reading your most recent play.

Years ago J. P. and Peggy McEvoy often traveled abroad without the company of their small children, and it was the custom for the children to write daily letters to their parents. The McEvoys were in a Latin American country when the president of that country was shot and killed. He was a man with a rather lurid extramarital life, and so when little Peggy's letter came it somehow seemed most appropriate. It said:

Oh — do write and tell us all about the assassignation!

A mother in Tampa, Florida, has sent along a poem written by her eight-year-old daughter, titled simply "History." It follows:

> Culumbus was smart
> To cross the sea
> To find our land
> He was famous to be
> The winds tossed the boat
> The sea was mean
> But truly then
> There was land to be seen
> He saw our home
> Our very old home
> And landed his boat
> Then went alone
> To red men wraped in wool and
> To their leader
> Cheif Sitting Bull

Mrs. Eleanor C. Stivison, a fifth-grade teacher at Uniondale, New York, has sent me an essay by one of her beatnik boy pupils. It follows:

My ambition

I'm go to be a engineer when I grove up. I want to be the engineer to rided on all the train that come and also go sometimes. I like to pull the string for the whisling. I also like to seat in the engineer seat, because sometimes it is soft and also cold.

Ruth W. Withers, a teacher in West Virginia, informs me that once a boy in her class was taking a test in world history. He came to this question: "What was the connection between ancient Greece and the Olympics?" His written answer: "They were friends."

All over the nation the youngsters continue to publish their own little newspapers and magazines. I have, for example, Vol. IV, No. VII, of the *Demington Officil Weird Tales,* printed in pencil in Cleveland. The editors, for some reason, have asked me not to use their names or the names of the people they have written about. Cagey about libel suits, probably. Here are three brief items from their journal:

Partys

The M.'s had a Halowen Party. The R.'s had one too. Partys are good ecept when there too noisy.

Stupid Sistrs

My sistr is a nut. So is Bobs. They are nincompups. We dont let them in are rooms ever.

Cigrets

Many people smoke cigerets. They are bat. Cigrets hurt your lungs mently, morly and phisicilly.

One of my own favorite juvenile newspapers is the *Fenelon Place Journal,* which has long been an institution in the family of Richard Bissell, the novelist and playwright. The editor is Tom Bissell, but the entire family participates and the subscription list is a roster of celebrities in the theater, the movies, and contemporary literature. Here is a travelogue written by Sam Bissell, age seven:

May 1959 we went to pick up Nat and went on to Maine. We got there at 6:00. We went on an xscrchin to Sqrrel Island and back on a boat. We toasted marchmellows over the fire for Break fast and dinner and lunch and snack and for popcorn. Edw. Chalmers & Johnny Bissell came to see us in a jag. Edw. said that he could ride the car across the footbrege. But he Didn't go a cross the footbrege. Then we went to get tom but we had neat hot dogs at Brunswick first. And pink milk. And a crab bit Papa's toe.

Finally a letter which should convince any doubter that a child's chief interest is not literature, but food. Rufus Blair of Hollywood has sent me this note, written by Hungry Kathy Ryan when she was seven:

Dear Mother, it is very bad for a child to be hungry at 25 to 8 so if you mind would you please get dinner on the table. and if you

169

would I would be very happy. You no that children that are hungry die. you read in the paper that most of the children die of under-feeding so please feed me. you no that sometimes the cat gets more than me. and I got very mad at you when you get impatient, you get so impatient that I am nervus. so I hope I get my dinner soon.

your friend Kathy Ryan.

Mr. Blair tells me that today Kathy is nineteen, a handsome ballet dancer of exquisite form and strong as a Percheron, so she must have gotten her dinner. There is value in protest.

28. THE SILENT TREATMENT

UP TO NOW this book has been concerned, in large part, with the usage and misusage of language. As a concluding exercise, let us consider the negative side of things — the *non*usage of language. I am inspired by the fact that my neighbors, Bob and Liz Gaffney, are not speaking to each other again, which means that all's right with the world.

This last time they went for seven straight weeks speaking to each other, saying, "Yes, dear," and "May I help you to some more potatoes, love?" and "Listen, you louse, quit acting like you were the All-Wise." Somehow, life is much duller in our neighborhood when Bob and Liz are on speaking terms. We thought it would never end, and then a day or so ago they resumed giving each other the silent treatment.

This is the way it came about: Bob has a habit of wiggling his foot whenever he's reading the newspaper. He crosses his right leg over his left knee, and as he reads, he moves his right foot back and forth in a sort of continuing twitch. When he came home from the office the other night he and Liz were on excellent terms. They chatted about the day's events all through dinner, and then Bob sat down to read.

"Quit wiggling your foot," Liz suddenly said.

Bob looked up from his paper, momentarily confused. "What's that?" he asked.

"I said," Liz told him, "quit wiggling your damfool foot."

"I didn't know I was wiggling it," said Bob, "but if I was, I can't see that it's any concern of yours. It's my foot and I'll wiggle it to suit myself."

"If you only knew," said Liz, "just how maddening it is. You sit there and wiggle that foot until I could scream. Why don't you get control of yourself?"

"I'm in perfect control of everything, including my foot," said Bob. "It so happens that I get a certain amount of pleasure out of wiggling my feet. It relaxes my shins. I like it."

Liz stood up, her eyes narrowed. "A typical excuse," she said. "Who ever heard of anybody having tense shins! Well, you can wiggle your foot off at the hinges for all I care. But you'll wiggle it without me!"

She marched out of the house, got into the car, and drove over to spend the evening with us.

I didn't attempt to lecture her. I didn't tell her that she should be more tolerant of Bob's wiggling foot, because I get a certain amount of enjoyment out of people who are Not Speaking to Each Other.

I have been interested in this aspect of human relationship for a long time. A dozen years ago I worked on the staff of a New York newspaper and one of my good friends was the paper's drama critic. One afternoon I was walking down the hallway that led to the locker room. My friend, the drama critic, was coming toward me. As we neared each other, I said, "Hi, Doug." He stared straight ahead and hurried past me. At first I thought he was merely in the grip of a horrifying hangover. A few minutes later I walked over to his desk in the city room. He didn't look up from his typewriter, and I asked him if he wanted to sneak out and have a couple at Nick's. He still didn't look up. "What's eating you?" I wanted to know. He continued typing, so I went back to my desk and thought about it awhile, and then wrote him a note, asking for an explanation. A copy boy handed the note to him, and without reading it, he tore it into bits.

He never spoke to me again. In the beginning I spent hours trying to figure it out. I had not done a single thing I could think of that would cause him to quit speaking. I had a mutual friend approach him, to ask what was troubling him. He said, "Don't mention that scum's name in my presence."

I left the paper, still unspoken to, and not long after that he died suddenly, and now I'll never know. Or maybe I shall know. If my evil life transports me to his place of residence in the hereafter, the first thing I'm going to say to him on arrival is, "Hey, why did you quit speaking to me?" The chances are he won't even look up from his shoveling.

A few years later I became acquainted with Bob and Liz Gaffney. In this couple I found the art of Not Speaking brought to its finest flower. I didn't realize just how expert Bob and Liz were until the trip to New England. The four of us decided to take a vacation together driving through New England. I did the driving and Bob usually sat alongside me while the two women occupied the back seat. We were in various hotels and motor courts and restaurants; we visited historical sites; we played some tennis, and stopped once to bowl, and did some swimming. We were together almost constantly for eight days, and I thought we had a fine, congenial time of it. It wasn't until after our return home that my wife and I found out that Bob and Liz had not spoken to each other throughout that trip.

We sat down, after we found it out, and retraced our journey, remembering every detail, and the more we thought about it, the more astonishing it became. We knew, of course, that the

Gaffneys sometimes went for two or three weeks without speaking at home. But that involved, as a general rule, only the evening hours and week ends. On the trip they were in each other's presence twenty-four hours a day, for eight days, without speaking a word to each other, and the important thing was that they didn't speak with such finesse that we didn't know it. That's art.

The technique of Not Speaking has never, to my knowledge, been adequately investigated by sociologists or psychologists. Being interested in the subject, I have for several years been conducting quiet observations, with special reference to the rules of the game. I've found out that there are few husbands and wives who don't quit speaking now and then. And the number of people who live in the same neighborhood and don't speak is beyond calculation. In my own bailiwick I know of two businesses where the partners carry on from day to day, month after month, without speaking to each other. In a nearby village there are two brothers who are business competitors and whose stores are directly across the street from each other. They have not spoken for thirty years. I have tried to find out what started it, but I get conflicting stories. The most sensible version is as follows:

Thirty years ago, when the brothers were boys, their mother forbade them to enter a certain poolroom. One day the younger of the two crept into the forbidden resort and found his brother already there, playing pool with a town character. The younger brother said, "Shoot me a game when you get through will you?" The older brother said, "You get the dickens out of here; you're too young." So the younger brother went home and said, "Mamma, Joe he's down in the poolroom." And when Joe came home his mother gave him what-for. After the yelling had died down, Joe turned on his younger brother and said, "You little tattletale twerp, I'll never speak to you again as long as I live!" It's beginning to look as if he'll make it.

I have read about a man named George Smith who works in box offices at various sporting events around New York and who quits speaking to people wholesale. Each Christmas he sends out calendars to all his acquaintances. Across the top of the calendar is printed: "I am not speaking to the following persons —"

Underneath is a list of the proscribed, perhaps two dozen altogether. The names on the list change from year to year, although I've noticed that there are a few individuals who seem to have permanent listing.

This George Smith sits in his box office and people line up in front of him for the purpose of buying tickets. Some of the individuals whose names appear on his calendar must surely show up before his wicket from time to time. He has to deal with them. I have no direct knowledge about it, but I can imagine how he manages it. His adversary stands face to face with him and asks for certain seat locations.

"Two in Section C, down front," says the adversary.

If George Smith has the requested seats, he can simply shove the tickets over the counter. His adversary either knows the price already or can look on the ticket for it. He lays down his money, George Smith gives him his change, and George has never uttered a word. His honor is intact.

Let us suppose, however, that the requested tickets are not available. How should George handle it? Could he scribble a note? He could not. Note writing is as flagrant a violation of the rules as is actual talking. Could he simply shake his head from side to side? He could not. Head shaking is out. George can do one of two things: He can sit there like a bump on a log, saying nothing, acting as if he didn't hear, hoping that his adversary will be smart enough to ask for seats in another location. Barring that, George can direct his gaze past his adversary and speak to the person next in line, saying, "Hey, you in the checkered shirt. If you're looking for seats in Section C, down front, there ain't any more. Might fix you up with good seats in Section F." This may be confusing to the man in the checkered shirt, but it gets George Smith off the hook. His adversary takes the seats in Section F.

There are many stories about people in the theatrical world who quit speaking to each other privately, but who are required to talk each other half to death onstage. I have heard of vaudeville teams whose two members carry on hilarious conversations on the stage every day, but once they walk through the wings they wouldn't speak to each other if their toenails were pulled out with chilled pincers. The same thing is true in the legitimate theater, where a man and a woman will go through torrid love scenes before the audience while giving each other the silent treatment elsewhere. It even happens in the world of sports. It is recorded that the late John McGraw, as manager of the New York Giants, was not on speaking terms with Charlie Herzog, his third baseman. If Mr. McGraw had some message to convey to Mr. Herzog, he did it through a third person, and Mr. Herzog conveyed his answer, if any, via the intermediary. Once during a tight and exciting game Mr. McGraw forgot himself when Mr. Herzog was at bat, and yelled a single word straight at him. "Bunt!" Mr. Herzog promptly swung hard and hit a home run.

Mr. Herzog said later that he had chosen to be insubordinate because Mr. McGraw had no moral right to address a direct remark to him.

Bob and Liz Gaffney, however, remain the chief source of my information on the art of Not Speaking. One Saturday afternoon a few months back, I went over to the Gaffneys' and found Bob sitting on his terrace smoking a cigar and glaring at grass.

"Where's Liz?" I asked him.

"Don't know," he said. "She drove off an hour ago. I imagine she's gone to get her hair done. We're going to dinner at the Mangans' tonight. We're Not Speaking."

"You people sure do a lot of Not Speaking," I ventured.

"Sure," he agreed. "Why not?"

"It's not quite civilized," I said. "It's not mature."

"Don't be silly," said Bob. "Not Speaking is the greatest weapon the human race has ever devised for itself. I think maybe you confuse Not Speaking with sulking. That's a mean, moody sort of thing — sulking. Not Speaking is a coldly calculated business. It can drive people out of their minds if it's handled properly."

"How long have you two been Not Speaking this time?"

"Started day before yesterday," he said, and then, almost to himself, he added admiringly, "Lord, how that woman can Not Speak!"

I told him I didn't see how they could carry on their day-by-day affairs without speaking. He said it's like everything else — all a matter of practice. He verified my notion that there are certain hard-and-fast rules that must be observed — such as the interdiction against writing notes and head nodding or head shaking.

"It's the same as in international law," he said. "You've got to have rules and mutual agreements in conducting a war. In Not Talking, it's no problem at all when there's a third party present. You simply make your feelings known with declarative sentences, addressed to the third party. But where the two of you are alone together, the thing would be most difficult if there weren't certain rules. Neither Liz nor I would ever stoop to note writing. Yet there's a way of communicating by writing that's perfectly legitimate."

He said that Liz had given a demonstration of it a couple of hours earlier. She had brought some stationery and a fountain

176

pen out to the terrace where Bob was sitting. She sat down and began writing, murmuring the lines to herself, as follows:

"Dearest Mother: We are all well physically, but I think Bob is mentally sick. He acts like a beast at times. But don't worry — this is my cross and I will bear it. Do you remember the Mangans? They are *so* nice. They have invited us to dinner tonight and I think it should be fun. I may have told you once about the Mangans and how peculiar they are about people being on time for dinner. They are serving tonight at seven-thirty and that means we should be there on the dot. I'm going to wear my new evening gown, the chartreuse I wrote you about. Well, I'll have to cut this short, as I'm expecting the man to repair the TV any minute, and I think Bob wants to talk to him about it. Your devoted daughter, Elizabeth."

"You see how much she accomplished?" said Bob. "She didn't say a word to me — just sat there talking out the letter to her mother — and she managed to let me know that we're supposed to go to the Mangans' for dinner, that we're supposed to be there at seven-thirty, that we're supposed to dress up a bit, and that I shouldn't leave the house because the TV repairman was coming."

"Marvelous!" I exclaimed. "But how did you let her know you'd go to the Mangans'? Or did you?"

"If I hadn't intended going," he said, "I'd have thrown back my head and laughed diabolically. Diabolical laughter doesn't constitute speaking, yet in a way it is more effective than speaking. However, it happened that I wanted to go to the Mangans'. Now, you see that bush right over there?"

I saw it. Bob said he waited a few minutes after Liz had finished murmuring the letter to her mother. Then he got up and walked over toward the bush and said:

"Well, hello there, little bird. What are you doing frisking around on a hot day like this? You better go on home to your mamma. We're going to leave later on today, going out to dinner about seven-fifteen, and we don't want you fooling around the house while we're away."

That did it. "She knew," said Bob, "that I was willing to go, and she knew what time we'd leave the house. She got right up and went inside, and I heard her on the telephone. It happens I don't know who she was calling, but I'm almost certain it was the hairdresser. Incidentally, the telephone is a great help."

"Yes, I know," I said. I could remember many times when one or the other of them had called us. If it was Bob calling he'd usually speak to me, while Liz would talk to my wife. If we hadn't known about their habits, we'd have thought sometimes that they had gone crazy. I would be summoned to the phone and Bob would say to me, without any preliminaries, "Hey, I just wanted to let you know that if my idiot wife has lamb one more time for dinner this week, I'm going to take a club and part her hair with it."

That sort of thing.

Sitting that afternoon on the terrace, Bob observed that the rules for Not Speaking are pretty well standardized.

"We've learned one important thing recently," he said. "It's permissible to make faces. You can't make a face at the other person. You make it without facing them. The most popular face is the one registering disgust. Like this."

He shrugged up his shoulders a bit and then contorted his face in a most eloquent manner. The expression clearly said, "Such colossal stupidity! To think that I'm saddled with this horrible creature for the rest of my natural life! How I'd love to bust her one!"

"Sometimes," Bob explained, "you have to hold it for quite a while. If I'm making that face, I make it at right angles to Liz, and if she doesn't happen to be looking in my direction, I have to hold it till I feel she does see it. I might add that there are legitimate ways of attracting her attention. Grunts, snorts, and

178

whinnies are allowable sounds, perfectly proper, and most effective at times. Just a couple of evenings ago I was sitting in the —"

We heard a car approaching and Liz drove up, her hair freshly set, as Bob had guessed. She got out of the car and came up on the terrace.

"Hi," she said to me. She didn't look at Bob, and Bob didn't look at her.

"Do you know anything about electricity?" she asked.

"Only that it makes lights turn on."

"Oh, that's too bad," she said. "We've got a fuse blown out in the basement; I thought you might be able to fix it."

I started to say I could replace a fuse, and then I realized that she was talking to Bob, through me. He groaned, and then whinnied, and went into the house, and I heard him clumping down the basement stairs. He was back in a few moments, and I got up to leave.

"Tell your wife," he said, "if you're on speaking terms with her, that I can't come up tomorrow to get that magazine she told me about. I'm leaving tomorrow morning for Pittsburgh on business. Be back Tuesday night, La Guardia Airport, Flight 402, arrival 9:12 P.M., Eastern Standard Time. Tell her I'll pick up the magazine later in the week."

So I went home and, in a fairly loud voice, gave that information to the dog.